Harnessing Uncertainty to Lead with Impact

BRILLIANT
DOUBT

JENNY WILLIAMS, MCC

First published in Great Britain by Practical Inspiration Publishing, 2026

© Jenny Williams, 2026

The moral rights of the author have been asserted.

ISBN   9781788606455 (paperback)
       9781788606448 (hardback)
       9781788606479 (ebook)

EU GPSR representative: LOGOS EUROPE, 9 rue Nicolas Poussin, LA ROCHELLE 17000, France Contact@logoseurope.eu

Want to bulk-buy copies of this book for your team and colleagues? We can customize the content and co-brand *Brilliant Doubt* to suit your business's needs.

Please email info@practicalinspiration.com for more details.

Practical Inspiration
Publishing

When I first worked with Jenny over 15 years ago, I was at a crossroads – uncertain, second-guessing, and tempted to play safe. Her ability to help me face my doubts head-on gave me the clarity and courage to make one of the most important decisions of my career: the leap from being an employee to co-founding my own company in China. That decision transformed my trajectory, and it was only possible because Jenny helped me see that doubt could be a signal, not a stop sign. In *Brilliant Doubt*, she distils the essence of that coaching into a powerful framework every leader can use. This book is both deeply practical and deeply human – a guide to turning doubt into the engine of wiser leadership.

Elisa Harca,
Co-Founder and CEO, Red Ant Asia (www.redantasia.com)

At a time when certainty is overvalued, *Brilliant Doubt* offers a bold and refreshing perspective. Jenny Williams reveals doubt not as a weakness, but as a hidden source of insight and strength. Through her exploration of self-doubt, situational doubt, and systemic doubt, she brings new understanding to how doubt shows up – and how it can serve us. With clarity, compassion, and practical wisdom, she shows how leaders can transform uncertainty into wiser choices, stronger relationships, and more authentic leadership. This is an essential companion for anyone who has ever quietly wondered, 'Am I enough?'

Jo Hicks,
Chief People Officer, NHS

Jenny was the first coach I ever brought into my leadership world, and she remains a trusted partner many years on. She brings energy, insight, and real curiosity to every conversation. *Brilliant Doubt* distils what I have seen repeatedly in practice: when leaders learn to work with doubt, they unlock clearer thinking, stronger relationships and more confident action.

Rachael Sansom,
CEO, UK & Europe, Havas Red

What stands out in *Brilliant Doubt* is the depth that comes from years of coaching those at the sharp edge of leadership. Jenny turns what many would see as a taboo into a force for good; this is a refreshing perspective on how understanding doubt can actually strengthen judgement, confidence, and connection.

Jonathan Lewis-Jones,
Executive Director, WPP Media

Jenny, I've followed your journey with Brilliant Doubt since our early conversations about the courage to question – something leaders rarely discuss openly. Your work reframes uncertainty as a strategic asset, transforming doubt into the clarity that drives better decisions and more authentic leadership. It's a timely and important contribution.

Martha Velando,
Global Marketing & Retail Strategy
Experience with P&G, L'Oréal, Coty, DeBeers, and Puig

In business, as in AI, intelligence starts with asking better questions. *Brilliant Doubt* shows leaders how to transform uncertainty into sharper decisions and bold action.

David Benigson,
CEO and Founder, Signal AI

Jenny's reframing of doubt is at once immensely thought-provoking and practical. With AI revolutionizing our world of work, professional doubt is growing exponentially. A guide on 'how to hold space for doubt' has never been more timely and relevant for today's leaders.

Carol Stickler,
Global Consulting Principal, Ogilvy North America.

Most leadership thinking avoids self-doubt altogether. *Brilliant Doubt* goes further. Jenny shines a light on the importance of giving voice not only to self-doubt but to situational and systemic doubt, the external forces that should equally demand our attention. This wider lens is exactly what leaders need to navigate complex organizational realities with sharper insight and wiser confidence.

Julie Davidson,
CMO and Advisor, formerly Chief Marketing and Communications Officer at London Business School

Brilliant Doubt is a powerful and practical exploration of doubt as a leadership strength. By naming and normalizing doubt, this book gives leaders a toolkit for navigating uncertainty with clarity and confidence.

Fiona Alderman,
Director of Legal and Governance,
London Borough of Haringey

Brilliant Doubt flips the script on traditional leadership and is a refreshing reminder that real strength in leadership doesn't come from unshakable certainty, but from the courage to embrace doubt.

In celebrating doubt as a superpower, it highlights the importance of questioning assumptions in a fast-changing world and offers genuine food for thought – perhaps the most resilient leaders are not those who claim to have all the answers, but those who remain open to new ones?

Jane McNeill,
COO, IAB UK

Brilliant Doubt has helped me see doubt as a valuable source of data that I now actively use to drive growth, both professionally and personally. It reminded me that doubt can be a healthy and powerful source of insight – one that fuels curiosity, learning, and reflection. This book offered fresh perspectives and practical tools for using doubt more intentionally and effectively.

Veronica Flyckt,
VP Data Excellence Center, KPN Netherlands

In a world where we may know we aren't the person in the room with all the answers, and may not dare say it, Jenny's book offers ways to grab on to doubt with both hands and say that we have doubt and that it's a good thing. A must-read for leaders. And for coaches.

Claire Pedrick,
Author of *Simplifying Coaching* and
The Human Behind the Coach

If you have ever doubted yourself, buy this book and celebrate!!

After reading this book you will, without doubt, embrace doubt, and value its power. In this brilliant book, Jenny's counterintuitive perspective makes the case for brilliant doubt. Jenny reframes doubt as a leader's greatest asset and introduces us to The Paradox of Doubt. The greater the success, the greater the doubts... certainty is not all it's cracked up to be.

Doubt is data we can do something with. Doubt offers hope.

Roger Fielding,
BSc PGCE MEd MPhil MBA MCC ICF MCC
Master Coach, Tutor, Cambridge University Coaching
Programmes, Fellow of the Association for Coaching

If in doubt, shout! Leaders thrive on doubt and embrace the challenges it projects. *Brilliant Doubt* is an all-comprehensive read which gives leaders the actionable tools to deal with uncertainty.

Henk Van Hulle,
CEO, Open Banking

Leaders who pretend they have all the answers rarely do. *Brilliant Doubt* hands us something far more powerful: the confidence to question, to challenge, to stay curious. Jenny brings doubt out of the shadows and into the spotlight, turning it into rocket fuel for bold decisions and brave leadership. This book crackles with energy and purpose. Read it. Use it. Then go shake up your organization.

Tony Miller,
CMO, Direct Line Group and Board Chair
of the Data Marketing Association (DMA)

For my brilliant brother, Jonathan

Contents

Part 4: Systemic doubt

Introduction: Why we need to talk about doubt

In a world that champions certainty, doubt is the enemy. An enemy best dismissed and avoided. Organizations want leaders who project certainty, whilst demanding authenticity from them. Leaders are asked to balance on a precarious tightrope between certainty and doubt. A challenging double bind.

But what if doubt is our greatest untapped asset?

What if doubt is the partner certainty needs?

Doubt is everywhere – quiet, constant, and often concealed.

In the boardroom, it shows up in unspoken thoughts: 'Am I really good enough to be here?'

In leadership, it's in the challenging questions: 'Is this the right decision?'

And in systems, it's in the silence when promotions favour some, and exclude others.

As an Executive Coach, I meet doubt every day – in high-achieving, smart, passionate people. We think doubt is a flaw to overcome.

But what if it's the very source of our integrity, creativity, and brilliance?

'I think I need to leave my role and work in a coffee shop instead. I constantly feel like I am going to fail. I am not in control. The leadership team will eventually work out I am dropping balls. Plus, I will get to spend more time with my two-year-old daughter.' These were the weighted words of doubt from a newly appointed Finance Director. She was serious about leaving. Serious about the coffee shop. And seriously good at her job. Yet, clouded by her own self-doubts, she could not see it. She doubted she was good enough, compared herself unfavourably to her peers, and questioned whether she could be the mum she wanted to be. The demons of doubt were vocally at play.

It took her 18 months to leave.

But not to the coffee shop – to a bigger role: Group Finance Director.

Brilliant progress, but what happened? Were her doubts a help or a hindrance?

She is not alone. Like the Vice President, trying to figure out his team restructure: 'I am going to have to restructure and reduce my direct reports from ten to seven. The person who would be best at running one part of the technology operation is technically great but I don't trust him. He is an inveterate gossiper, with form for leaking things upwards as well as downwards. What if I make the wrong call?'

Or the Project Manager, reflecting on the silence she is encountering: 'It is like everyone has drunk the Kool-Aid, no one is pushing back. We don't have the time or the resources to deliver what is required, outside of the big meetings people say it is impossible, but then when we are all together nothing is said.'

The whispers of doubt

Doubt will quietly whisper:

- 'What if I mess this up?'

- 'What if the team does not deliver?'

- 'What if my line manager doesn't fight for me at the promotion panel?'

- 'Why am I the only one who is not sure?'

- 'What is the point in voicing my concerns? They are never listened to.'

A spiralling conversation, often leading nowhere. In our work lives doubt often manifests as the imposter, as we nervously wait to see if others see the doubt that we see in ourselves. Unsurprisingly, we try to banish it, or at best ignore it by 'embracing the fear and doing it anyway'. And why not? It can be uncomfortable – creating a busy mind, a racing heart, and a stuck body. Frozen. Sometimes our doubt is obvious. But sometimes it is not – if we are not doubting on the outside, we are likely doubting on the inside. Doubt wears a mask, leaking out in other ways – perfectionism, or an inability to delegate or micromanage. Doubt is the chameleon, morphing to keep a seat at our table.

But what if this chameleon has more to offer us?

My coaching clients nearly always say at some point, 'I suffer from imposter syndrome.' People want a 'cure'; there is an implicit ask – 'can you help me get rid of it?' For years I have privately called my clients something else: *the brilliant doubters*. Like the public sector CEO who found it hard to speak in rooms with her peers, yet led an organization of 1,800 people. Or the Director who would minimize what he was saying by adding a caveat alongside his recommendation – 'Having said all that, I might be wrong.' And yet his 360-feedback said, 'He is the best in our business globally (in his area of specialism). The only person who does not see how amazing he is, is himself.' A brilliant doubter.

The paradox of doubt: some of the most successful people are also the biggest doubters. But what if it's their doubt that helps make them successful?

As Jacinda Ahern reflected in her book *A Different Kind of Power*:

> 'If you have impostor syndrome, or question yourself, channel that.... In fact, all of the traits that you believe are your flaws will come to be your strengths. The things you thought would cripple you will in fact make you stronger, make you better.... They will give you a different kind of power, and make you a leader that this world, with all its turmoil, might just need.'[1]

There is a duality to doubt. To date we have had a one-sided conversation with it. The side which focuses on its rumination and stuckness. Yes, it can paralyze, but it can also unlock. All change starts with a doubt – *what if this can be better?* Doubt poses the question – 'what if?' Progress starts with doubt: if we don't doubt, we are accepting the status quo. It opens the door to possibility – a place for change, creativity, and courage. A place for progression.

And right now, organizations urgently need change, creativity, and courage.

Living the paradox of doubt and certainty

We live in a world where equal measures of doubt and certainty are not only inevitable – but essential.

This is the contradiction of our time: faced with profound uncertainty about our climate, global stability, the advancement of AI, and our anxious and overstretched humanity, we cling to certainty. Certainty that we find in ideologies, whether left or right. Certainty found in hardened positions, especially online, where nuance disappears.

We see this contradiction playing out in organizations too. As businesses undergo relentless transformation, leaders tighten their grip. Power struggles emerge. Silos deepen. We harden ourselves to protect. How have we arrived at this moment – an age so shaped by doubt, yet obsessed with projecting certainty?

The answer may be this: certainty has become a mask. A defence against the discomfort of not knowing. But in today's complex world, what we need isn't more certainty. We need a deeper relationship with doubt.

Meanwhile, organizations have avoided this deeper relationship with doubt, but other disciplines have not. Doubt is the fuel of science, the arts, psychology, and philosophy. There is wisdom to be gained from their workings with doubt, which we will explore further.

Professionally, we need to do doubt differently

We need to 'do' doubt in business. By acknowledging it and inviting it to the table; asking its opinion and valuing its insight. We need the confidence to trust that doubt has something meaningful to contribute to the individual, the situation, and the organization. But only if we let it speak. Doubt is the grit in the oyster – essential for creation.

Professional Doubt

To 'do' doubt, we need to start by naming it – to surface it.

The current definition of doubt is insufficient. The dictionary defines doubt as 'a feeling of uncertainty or lack of conviction.'[2]

This definition is too limited; it is a broad, sweeping description focusing only on the side of doubt that is 'lacking.' It does not cover the detail, the nuance, and the benefit that doubt can have in a professional context. It needs to evolve.

Currently, our obsession is with our own internal self-doubt, but there are two other forms which don't get airtime, namely *situational* and *systemic* doubt. In a professional setting, doubt encompasses all three forms – in fact one often begets another.

Doubt is the grit in the oyster – essential for creation.

The types of Professional Doubt:

- *Self-doubt* is our internal dialogue about ourselves – our abilities, value, or legitimacy. Imposter syndrome is a common form of self-doubt.

- *Situational doubt* is a specific, tangible doubt that sits outside of us, such as questioning the reliability of data or the dynamics of a relationship.

- *Systemic doubt* is a more intangible doubt that arises from the wider system – its values, behaviours, power structures, and the invisible architecture that shapes what is seen, said, and done.

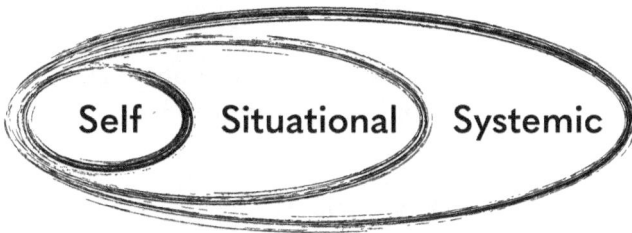

Figure 1: The three forms of Professional Doubt

They are distinct, but interconnected – just as when we experience different kinds of weather:

- *Self-doubt*: how does the weather make you feel? How does it affect your mood?

- *Situational doubt*: when you look at the weather what can you see outside? Is it raining? What colour is the sky?

- *Systemic doubt*: what is driving the weather patterns? Is this dry spell created by the southerly winds from the continent?

Like weather systems, these doubts influence and amplify each other. And like weather, there's a quiet beauty in them, if we pay attention. The beauty comes from actively engaging with it, so that it works on our behalf.

Active Doubt: the force that makes doubt work

I call this Active Doubt: doubt that is no longer passive or paralyzing, but alert, intentional, and constructive. The useful side of doubt, the doubt we need to get to better.

Doubt can surface what's been overlooked, unspoken, or dismissed. I think of it like a web. Webs aren't just beautiful; they have a purpose: to catch what might otherwise go unseen. That's what doubt does when it's active.

Active Doubt drives change, collaboration, courage, and creativity. It moves us from being *doubtful* to becoming *doubt fuelled*, where doubt becomes a source of energy, not a barrier.

The mission of this book is to rethink doubt – and reclaim its power to help us lead better in this complex age.

Owning my own doubt

This book has been a labour of doubt – written slowly over two years, through more hesitation than momentum. As someone who has spent thousands of hours coaching leaders at the highest levels, I know how doubt shows up in others. But this book asked me to confront how it shows up in me.

I could list my credentials: nearly two decades as an executive coach, a thriving business built almost entirely on referrals, and clients that include FTSE 100 leaders and public service CEOs. But none of that stopped me from wondering: *who am I to write this book?*

At my publisher's author day, I met a writer who finished their book in three weeks. Meanwhile, the 'doubt coach' was still tangled in her first draft after two years. You couldn't make it up.

What I haven't doubted is my curiosity about others. I've had no trouble seeking out stories, conducting interviews, or drawing insights from conversations. But when it came to my own voice on the page, I stalled. It was easier to hide – something I've mastered over years of creating space for others. The hand on my clients' backs as they step forward. And that worked – until now.

Writing this book meant becoming visible in a way I've avoided. It meant being seen and potentially judged. That's my version of doubt.

I coached a creative once who was afraid to exhibit their work. 'It's a window into my mind', they said. I understood completely. This book is mine.

You are holding the result. Whether doubt hindered or helped, I'll let you decide.

Doubt: the path we will take

We will start by exploring why we need doubt now in organizations and leadership. Then, we will dive deeper into each of the three forms of doubt: defining each of them, making the case for their brilliance, before showing how to turn them into something useful.

By making doubt active,
It becomes a force,
To create brilliance.

Meet the brilliant doubters

To make the case for doubt, I will introduce you to some of my coaching clients. Confidentiality is everything in coaching, so when I share client stories, I have changed perhaps their names, roles, and companies. But, the stories themselves are factually true. I share them to encourage you to rethink your own relationship with doubt.

Alongside my client stories are interviews with successful people who were incredibly generous with their time and provided insights to challenge and shape my thinking. If I have used their real name, they have been a generous individual who has shared their time and thinking with me. Thank you.

This book is for you, if you have ever doubted yourself, what is happening around you, or the system that you are in. It is for those who are tired of pretending that doubt does not exist, and are ready to lead differently. Written by a fellow doubter, it is a call to arms – a hand on your back. We are in this together.

At this point, you don't have to believe you are brilliant – yet. But you do have to believe that doubt has something to teach you.

What if we started by doubting doubt itself?

Let's get curious.

Let's start there.

'Doubt is the origin of wisdom'

- René Descartes

part
one

The Case for Doubt

Chapter 1:
As doubt grows: is certainty the answer?

It is 30 April 2025, and I am writing this as London basks in 26 degrees – a rare burst of sunrays. This book is a conversation about doubt, and in the UK, no conversation is complete without mentioning our uncertain weather. We cope with the uncertainty, and the disappointment it often brings, by talking about it.

It's predictable uncertainty.

And yet, all around me is *un*predictable uncertainty.

On Monday, Spain and Portugal suffered massive power losses. The systems that function to keep daily lives running shut down, triggering shock, panic buying, and plans upended.

Meanwhile, British retailer Marks and Spencer has been riding high on the revitalization of its clothes offer – recently dubbed the 'new Zara.' Yet, they are currently experiencing a full-scale cyber-attack, forcing a pause in their entire online operation and losing approximately £3.8 million[1] in sales per day. Across the water, the unpredictable Trump administration continues to send tsunami-size waves throughout the world, impacting everyone from solo entrepreneurs to the tech giants of Apple as they grapple with this shifting landscape.

Closer to home, my clients are feeling their energy and resilience being tested by increasingly unrealistic demands from organizations. Even good news feels unpredictable: one client recently landed a long-overdue promotion, joyful and unexpected.

It might be beautiful outside today, but has there ever been a more chaotic, uncertain time?

No wonder we crave certainty.

But could this craving be blinding us to something more powerful?

Why certainty feels good

Imagine waking one morning to find a box sitting ominously outside your front door. Inside is a single piece of string – the length revealing the exact moment of your death. What would we do if our string were tragically short? Or even surprisingly long? How might that knowledge change the way we live?

This is the premise of *The Measure* by Nikki Erlick,[2] a novel that explores the greatest uncertainty we face – when are we going to die. How would we live if we had certainty about this ultimate unknown?

The Measure is fiction – but Bryan Johnson is attempting to make it real. The tech multi-millionaire spends $2 million a year in pursuit of reversing his biological age, becoming what some might describe as a real-life Benjamin Button. His goal is to extend his lifespan as far as science will allow. He is biohacking his way towards control over his own demise – the ultimate obsession. At the heart of both *The Measure* and Johnson's quest lie the same pursuit of certainty. But to what end? And at what cost?

Johnson's biohacking is a personal attempt to wrestle uncertainty into submission. But the search for certainty isn't only individual – it's collective. Human beings have always sought control through shared meaning, weaving stories and symbols to make sense of the unpredictable. Yuval Noah Harari captures this in *Sapiens: A Brief History of Humankind* (2011), in which he explores why *Homo sapiens* became the dominant species on earth. It was not because we were the strongest or smartest, but because of our unique ability to believe in and co-operate around shared fictions:

> *'Ever since the Cognitive Revolution, Sapiens have thus been living in a dual reality. On the one hand, the objective reality of rivers, trees and lions; and on the other hand, the imagined reality of gods, nations and corporations. As time went by, the imagined reality became ever more powerful, so that today the very survival of rivers, trees and lions depends on the grace of imagined entities such as the United States and Google.'*[3]

We have evolved to crave certainty. We create it through the stories we tell – through the interpretations and beliefs we put in place to construct our shared reality. It is this ability to imagine and agree upon fictions that has made us successful.

Our evolution has hard-wired storytelling into us to create certainty and ultimately survival.

Our evolutionary knack for shared storytelling also shapes how we process the world individually. Each of us builds certainty through the stories we tell ourselves. Even a single word can spark a flood of associations. Ask ten people what comes to mind when they hear the word 'dog', you would likely get ten different answers, ranging from fluffy, to loud, to Dalmatian, or in my case, rock star. Each answer reflects personal experience and feelings. Mine comes from my stubborn, scruffy four-legged 'rock star', named after one of my favourite singers.

Our minds are wired to make fast, instinctive judgments – drawing on emotions, memories, and impressions. It's how we make quick decisions about what we like, trust, or believe. This kind of thinking offers immediate certainty – even if it's not always accurate.

But we also have the capacity for slower, more deliberate thought. This mode requires effort: to pause, reflect, question. It's the part of us that notices nuance, spots contradictions, and asks: *could there be another way to see this?*

Certainty thrives in the fast lane. Doubt lives in the pause.

The problem with craving certainty

We fight and fudge doubt with certainty – pushing it away or leaving it to sit awkwardly in the corner of our minds. But what do we lose when certainty is our preference?

Certainty is a full stop. It requires effort to put the full stop in place, and even more effort to keep it there. Effort spent controlling things is wasted energy. Energy that is diverted away from possibility, from creating, and above all from learning. Effort that can increase our anxiety, by ceding to the false myth that we can control life. With control there is no hope, there is no possibility, and there is no growth.

Where in your life might your craving for certainty inadvertently be causing you challenges?

The three powerful currents

If certainty is hardwired, how do we cope when we are swimming in doubt, wearing our armbands of certainty to support and keep us afloat? These armbands show up in more ways than we think. As the world becomes more uncertain, we seem to become more certain. To stop ourselves drowning in doubt, do we cling tighter to the life raft of certainty? Is it a coping mechanism?

Take a digital stroll through X (formerly Twitter) and you will see people metaphorically shouting their certainty at each other – taking hard positions, defending beliefs with increasing intensity. But it's not just online. It's in friendship groups, workplaces, even leadership teams. Organizations set bold, ambitious targets their workforce may not be equipped to deliver, and don't listen to the pushback. Politicians promise impossibilities – President Trump claimed before he was elected, 'I will end the war in 24 hours.' We want to believe them – of course we do. *Certainty is seductive.*

But we keep reaching for black-and-white arguments, even as we live in a world that is swirling with complexity, that is reshaping its very relationship with truth. Facts are recast as falsehoods.

Truth is claimed by the individual. We are saturated in content – the amount and the speed at which it circles around us making it harder to decipher what is true, accurate, or even relevant. In our rush to make meaning, we fall back on simplicity. Yet meaning requires deeper listening and understanding – not harder certainty.

We are carried by three powerful currents of doubt: the person in doubt, the organization in doubt, and the world in doubt.

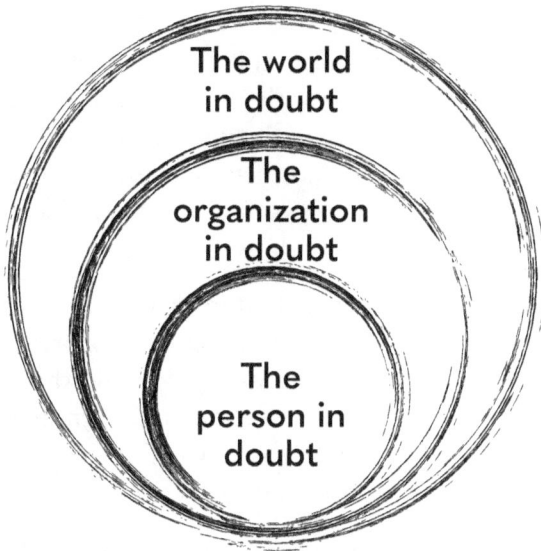

Figure 2: Three powerful currents

These currents form the foundation of how we experience and respond to doubt. They align closely with the three types of doubt explored throughout this book:

- *Self-doubt* arises within the person.

- *Situational doubt* emerges from a specific external situation, often shaped by the organizational context.

- *Systemic doubt* is provoked by unseen forces in the wider ecosystem.

As we try and stay afloat, what are we experiencing in the water?

1. The person in doubt

We try to avoid doubt, as our default is optimism: we think *it* might happen to *you*, but it is unlikely to happen to *me*. How else can we explain our willingness to marry despite high divorce rates, to drink alcohol despite overwhelming evidence of its health risks, or to continue with carbon-heavy lifestyles even though the science shows that change must be a collective effort? Tali Sharot, neuroscientist and Professor at University College London, describes optimists as: 'people who expect more kisses in their future, more strolls in the park. And that anticipation enhances their well-being.'[4] This optimism bias is the belief that the future will be better than the past or the present. We underestimate our personal risk and are selective in how we process information, often avoiding altogether the data that suggests that things are not a good idea. Optimism keeps us moving but it also blinds us to doubt.

It is therefore unsurprising that more people are turning away from the news. According to a report by Oxford University's Reuters Institute, 39% of people worldwide said they sometimes or often actively avoid the news, compared with 29% in 2017.[5] This is a protection strategy of sorts. An effort to protect oneself from challenging realities and beliefs.

In the west we have grown up in a largely safe world, with everything seeming to be getting better, but that's no longer the case for younger generations. Previously, there was an illusion of predictability and control, even though in reality this was not the case. As the external world becomes more doubtful and uncertain, it is natural to focus on the things we can control and actively seek out certainty.

By avoiding or hardening around our own certainties, our focus turns inward and onto ourselves. The digital world becomes a mirror for us. One that distorts the image we see of ourselves and distorts how we project out. Nothing is as it seems. We reside in digital echo chambers that confirm – or even fuel – our doubts. A toxic positivity where ever more perfect lives are portrayed, or the presented hero has overcome some challenge – which we can now do too (often with their help). We can easily miss the role of critical thinking, to challenge and provoke what we are being exposed to. It can be hard to do this, as the algorithms are working hard to keep the distortion in place.

The digital challenges are also acutely felt in the workplace – there are more ways people can be contacted and interrupted than ever before, increasing the feeling of being always on, always available, and always having to answer.

The impact on our well-being and mental health is clear. The Global Flourishing Study (2025)[6] looked at global well-being data from 22 countries and found that the U-shaped relationship between age and well-being, in which young people and people in later life used to report higher well-being than middle-aged adults, no longer holds true. Instead, they found that flourishing is flat until about age 50 and increases thereafter in Argentina, Australia, Brazil, Germany, Mexico, Spain, Sweden, the United Kingdom, and the United States.

Our openness to talking about how we are feeling, and particularly to having these conversations in the workplace, has grown. There is practical support, from Mental Health First Aiders to well-being courses; and changes in corporate policies to support employees with life challenges, from the focus on menopause, to carers support to help with fertility challenges. If we want healthier workplaces, we also need to legitimize doubt – not just as a feeling but also as an organizational response.

When the doubtful person is welcomed, it can lead to better questions, more effective collaboration, and more resilient decision-making.

2. The organization in doubt

In 2007, Nokia was riding high with a 38% share of the global market and €51 billion in sales. I was one of its 112,000 employees.[7] Of course, we know how the story ended: only six years later, Microsoft bought the Devices and Services division, and the once iconic Nokia brand quietly disappeared from consumer minds and hands, despite later attempts to revive it. Yet, when I joined, I never considered that the business could disappear. The unthinkable happened, and fast. Nokia joined a long list of once-dominant names that faltered or fell from their heights – Blackberry, Toys "R" Us, Yahoo, and WeWork. Tech, retail, and services – no sector is immune. Any business can be disrupted, disposed of, and disappear.

My experience at Nokia was a masterclass in leading through chaos. One minute we were the world's leading phone brand – the next, we were struggling to survive. It was my first real encounter with what many now call a VUCA world: one shaped by Volatility, Uncertainty, Complexity, and Ambiguity. VUCA became a popular way for organizations to make sense of fast-changing external conditions – shifting markets, global competition, emerging tech. But while it helped explain the turbulence outside, it didn't account for the human impact inside.

Enter BANI – a more modern lens. It stands for Brittle, Anxious, Nonlinear, and Incomprehensible. Whereas VUCA maps the environment, BANI explores how it feels to live and lead within it. It gives us a language for the internal impact: the doubts, the overwhelm, the sense that things could break at any moment.

Doubt lives in these fault lines. And when we name the patterns – brittle systems, anxious teams, unpredictable outcomes – we give ourselves permission to respond differently.

We'll explore this further in Chapter 9, but here, BANI helps us connect the dots: between global volatility, organizational fragility, and the very personal experience of doubt.

Falling levels of trust are another aspect of doubt. According to the 2025 Edelman Trust Index,[8] we are trusting institutions – including businesses – less, with trust dropping globally by three points in one year. Doubt inside organizations is growing, including whether they can still be counted on, particularly with job insecurity rising across the board.

The level of challenge to leaders to navigate through this is high.

In an age of doubt, we don't need louder certainty. We need leaders willing to listen, learn, and let go of their thinking to respond to new realities – even when it makes them look unsure. This is not weakness, this is wisdom.

3. The world in doubt

There is growing evidence that we are living in a more doubtful world.

The World Uncertainty Index[9] shows global measures of uncertainty have roughly doubled since 2000. The index is calculated by counting the percentage of instances of the word 'uncertain' (or its variant) in the Economist Intelligence Unit country reports. It draws a distinction between *risk* – situations where the outcome and probabilities are largely known, such as flipping a coin – and *uncertainty* – where the outcomes and probabilities are largely unknown, such as how the pandemic was going to unfold. This level of uncertainty influences decisions at all levels, from individual choices – 'should I leave my current job?', to corporate strategies – 'should we move our supply chain from China to Europe?' And whilst the unknowns are unknown, many can be labelled – the impact of AI, our vulnerability to climate change, how this will impact geopolitics, and where power is shifting in the world – changes that carry risk, but also the chance for reinvention. A chance to rethink what we value, and how we reinvent for the better.

In the 2025 Edelman Trust Barometer,[10] we see that the erosion of institutional trust is fuelling societal doubt. Traditional pillars of trust, such as government, business, and the media, are no longer perceived to be providing the guardrails that people expect. Trust in peer opinion now often outweighs the voices of experts, government, and the media, part-explaining the rise of non-traditional media. Creating a performative need for certainty, even when the truth is complex.

This may explain in part why politicians choose to answer complex questions in interviews with certainty – whether it is providing solutions to reducing immigration, the climate, or the cost-of-living crises. All systemic, complex, knotty issues. In a confused world, people connect with voices that feel right, rather than those that are factually right. Is this our politicians' fault, or have we trained them to provide our armbands?

Nowhere is this clearer than in the contentious debate on assisted dying in the UK, which is highly nuanced, personal and complex. Health Secretary Wes Streeting was originally in favour of assisted dying legislation and voted for it in a 2015 House of Commons debate. Yet, in October 2024 he opposed the Terminally Ill Adults (End of Life) Bill. 'I think that is a chilling slippery slope argument, and I would hate for people to opt for assisted dying because they think they're saving someone somewhere money, whether that's relatives or the NHS,'[11] he explained. His change in stance coincided with him taking on the role of Health Secretary. As Health Secretary, he likely encountered new data, competing priorities, or risks to vulnerable patients that shaped his revised position. We can agree or disagree with his position; I am not making an argument either for or against, but I am arguing that he needs to be able to doubt his original view – to take on board new data as and when it presents.

We need our political leaders to keep evolving their thinking and have a more nuanced debate, and this extends to the leaders of our organizations too. And what is our role in this? Perhaps it is not just about trusting more but asking better questions and becoming more comfortable with ambiguity. In ambiguity there is possibility, possibility that things can change for the better. It may mean letting go of the illusion of certainty – and learning to navigate without armbands.

The hope in doubt

Doubt is a seed of growth. When the seed is planted, it opens up to possibility, to change, and to hope. To doubt is an act of hope. A hope for better.

The Austrian philosopher Karl Popper argued that optimism is a moral duty. By combining hope with effort, we can help to progress society and overcome challenges. A belief that things can get better. There is an argument that optimism is even more of a moral duty in this uncertain world we now live in. Popper was not advocating blind optimism, an optimism that is not tethered to reality, or what is in front of the person. Instead, he wanted an optimism that meets the world where it is at. Meeting the world where it is at requires us to doubt too. We can doubt with optimism. This is not passive acceptance – it is active engagement. When we meet our world as it is, doubt becomes not our weakness, but our way forward.

Doubt challenges certainty with purpose – the purpose of seeking better.

Doubt distilled: is certainty the answer?

- *We are wired for certainty – but built to adapt.* Our brains favour quick answers and familiar stories, yet our evolution depends on our ability to respond to complexity, ambiguity, and change.

- *Certainty feels safe, but it comes at a cost.* It can blind us to nuance, silence other voices, and shut down learning. When certainty becomes a coping mechanism, it hardens into rigidity.

- *Doubt shows up when the world shifts – and it is shifting fast.* We live in an age of escalating uncertainty: geopolitical shocks, organizational fragility, and digital distortion all generate doubt. But that doubt is data – and ignoring it is risky.

- *In a BANI world, doubt is a leadership skill.* Brittle systems, anxious teams, nonlinear change, and incomprehensible complexity all demand a different way of thinking. Doubt helps us to slow down, question assumptions, and surface better paths forward.

- *Certainty closes. Doubt opens.* Certainty is a full stop. Doubt is a doorway – to better decisions, to deeper thinking, and to wiser leadership.

- *To doubt is to hope.* Doubt is not the opposite of optimism; it is its ally. When rooted in purpose, doubt becomes a creative force – not a weakness to be suppressed, but a strength to be cultivated.

We all doubt: but why do some harness it and others don't?

Chapter 2:
Doubt: a neglected discipline

We all doubt. And yet, in our organizational lives we push doubt down. If you have felt uneasy about a decision in a meeting but stayed silent, you already know what organizational doubt feels like. It is not abstract. It is embodied. We try to balance, often in silence, on the tightrope of doubt and certainty. But what if we did not have to? What if we brought doubt out in the open, treated it as a discipline, and reclaimed what it has to offer? Doubt would no longer be a hindrance, but a tool to work with.

Doubt and belief: the first story

One of the earliest stories of doubt is Adam and Eve. In the Garden of Eden, the serpent plants a seed of doubt in Eve's mind, questioning God's commandment not to eat from the tree. She disobeys Him and eats the forbidden fruit. The serpent's doubt challenges authority and trust, in this case becoming a catalyst for disobedience.

This story is known as the 'original sin', so perhaps it is not so surprising, after all, that we have a complicated relationship with doubt?

If you were to visualize this complicated relationship with doubt as a person, what would they look like?

The British sculptor Sir Antony Gormley imagined it as having a body that had collapsed into itself, and yet 'the head juts out enquiringly into space at large'. His angular DOUBT sculpture found its home at Wells Cathedral, Somerset for three years. DOUBT sat on a specially made plinth surrounded by an impressive array of medieval sculptures – Apostles, Saints, Kings and Bishops, the Virgin Mary, even Christ himself. All symbols of believing; and juxtaposed between these figures was DOUBT. It was visually arresting, conceptually challenging, and judging by the mixed reactions from the local community, literally challenging too.

'I am very aware of the paradox of placing an object called DOUBT on the façade of a building devoted to belief, but it seems to me that doubting, interrogating, questioning, are all part of belief,' Gormley said. 'For me doubt can be a positive force and the imaginative engine of future possibility.'[1]

Doubt and faith are intrinsically intertwined. As Chancellor James of Wells Cathedral emphasized, 'Doubt is not the opposite of faith, it is part of somebody's faith journey.'[2] Gormley described the sculpture as a 'grain of salt' in amongst the majesty of the Gothic building, a grain asking you to question and discover something deeper. That questioning is part of faith – who am I? Why am I here? Faith embraces doubt. It holds both certainty and uncertainty – metaphorically, it is a broad church.

We're used to thinking of belief as strength and doubt as weakness. But what if the real strength is being able to hold both? What if you could hold your belief in a project while listening openly to the doubts others have about it?

Brilliant doubter: Ahmed, lawyer

Faith is largely ignored in the workplace, but at times it can present itself like a 'grain of salt' and be keenly felt, particularly if the environment or people make it more challenging for a person to practice their faith. I coached a lawyer who was excellent at his job. He was talented, warm, funny, and a practising Muslim. The organization had a 'work hard, play hard' culture, where play was often washed down with alcohol. My client not only didn't drink but could not sit at the same table as alcohol either, making it difficult for him to socialize with the team. Despite enjoying it there, he wasn't sure if he fitted in, because of his faith.

He was an engaging presenter. When we looked closer, he realized it was his faith that made him good at presenting – every Friday evening he led teenage Muslims through their faith class. Teenagers can make mighty good hecklers, so he had to learn to think on his feet and find interesting ways to hold their attention. These young Muslims had made him a brilliant presenter. I asked him, 'what is the benefit of you being a Muslim for this company?' Silence followed, then he spoke at length about how his faith had made him a caring colleague, how it showed clients how the business embraced diverse thinking, and how people trusted him because of his strong ethics. If he hadn't doubted, he would not have understood what he and his faith uniquely bring to the organization. From his initial doubt came a deeper connection and engagement with why he worked in the business.

Discovery questions

If you have ever felt unsure whether you belong, you are not alone – but you may be sitting on overlooked strengths. By exploring what makes you feel different, you often discover what makes you distinctly valuable to the organization.

- What overlooked strengths might be hiding in the places you doubt yourself most?

- What would change if you looked at your difference as a strength?

What is doubt, really?

To go deeper in our thinking on doubt, we need to understand its linguistic roots. The word originated from the old French *doute* (noun) and *douter* (verb), which came from the Latin root *dubitare*, meaning to hesitate, waver, or be uncertain. This reflects our current understanding of it, but it goes further, because *dubitare* itself actually comes from *duo*, meaning two; so, to doubt means to be caught between two possibilities. It is neither negative nor positive, but reflects the duality of the word. It offers us the opportunity to embrace its duality again and embrace the dynamic tension it brings – in a helpful, constructive way.

It is no accident when we say we are in 'two minds' – doubt is literally divided thinking. But that split is not failure, it is about possibility waiting to be shaped.

When have you been in 'two minds' about a decision at work? What did you do as a result? How did each of those 'minds' help you to ultimately reach a better outcome?

Whilst many organizations don't naturally embrace or encourage this duality, it is central to the success of some disciplines, which offer us an alternative insight into what might be helpful.

Disciplines that embrace doubt: what can we learn?

Science: breakthroughs begin with doubt

Doubt is fundamental in science. It is both systematic and constructive: scientists move forward by examining their doubts, ruling things out, and reaching evidence-based conclusions. Doubt challenges and refines what is known knowledge, pushing knowledge forward.

Dr Heather Ang, a blood researcher, works to find breakthroughs to so-far-unfathomable diseases. Her approach is data-driven and objective; she described to me the scientist's mindset:

- There is no such thing as a failed experiment. The only failure is failing to learn something. Even a small insight will move the work forward.

- In science, you are rarely ever 'done'; there is always another variable.

- If you've reached a final truth, you've reached the end point – and the end point is rare.

Even when you are sure of something, uncertainty remains. Heisenberg's Uncertainty Principle[3] illustrates this: we cannot know both the speed and location of a particle at the same time. The more accurately one measures the speed, the more uncertainty there is of its location and vice versa. Certainty and uncertainty coexist – a duality.

In 2011, Italian scientists at the OPERA experiment reported that neutrinos appeared to travel faster than light, contradicting Einstein's theory of relativity.[4] The findings were announced before the peer review. Horror of horrors, it was later found that the results were due to a loose cable. Once the cable was tightened, Einstein's theory held. If only they had waited for the peer review process.

Peer review is a systemized process of doubt. Experts review, challenge, and critique each other's work to ensure it stands up.

It validates, corrects, and prevents flawed science from gaining traction. What if we borrowed from this systemized process of doubt, and used it to inspire better and more robust thinking? Where would your work benefit from a 'peer review' process?

Today, science is increasingly challenged – not just from within, but from society at large. Medical science, in particular, faces a wave of 'social review', casting doubt on the validity of vaccines, fluoride, and other long-established practices. Often, these doubts come from outside scientific expertise and are shaped by social media echo chambers. It is tempting to dismiss them.

But that is too simplistic. Doubt, even when it comes from outside the system, has often sparked necessary change. Rachel Carson in her book *Silent Spring* (1962) directly challenged the chemical industry, in turn, on the devastating impact of indiscriminate pesticide use (especially DDT) on ecosystems, wildlife, and human health. The chemical industry launched a massive campaign to discredit her, attacking her as an alarmist and unscientific. Fortunately they failed. It led to a nationwide ban on DDT and spurred the creation of the US Environmental Protection Agency.[5]

What's often missing in today's debates is space for nuance and uncertainty. Debates are reduced to binaries – yes or no, believer or sceptic, pro- or anti-. Winning replaces problem solving. But doubt – active, rigorous doubt – needs space to explore, not just to oppose.

This is where we can draw a distinction between scepticism and constructive criticism. A sceptic starts unconvinced and asks for evidence, and requires the other person to do the heavy lifting in providing it. Constructive criticism, however, comes from a place of shared purpose: *how can we make this better together?* It's collaborative rather than combative.

Science treats doubt as a discipline. It is how breakthroughs happen. So why is scientific uncertainty seen as rigour, while workplace uncertainty is undervalued? What if organizations treated uncertainty like scientists do – as something to test, learn from, and build on?

Philosophy: doubt as a partner searching for truth

René Descartes (1596–1650) is known as the father of modern philosophy. But perhaps more importantly, he is the forgotten forefather of doubt. The original brilliant doubter.

Before Descartes, knowledge was based on tradition, religion, and authority. He challenged this and viewed knowledge and beliefs as uncertain – open to doubt. He took this as far as he could, challenging his very existence, and only at that point did he concede there was no doubt that he did exist – 'Cogito, Ergo Sum,' or 'I think, therefore, I am.'[6] He argued that thinking and existing are one and the same thing. If someone is questioning their very existence, the fact that they can question it is evidence enough of their thinking.

His approach to this was 'methodic doubt,' a process for getting to the truth by systematically questioning everything he could possibly doubt, to uncover what could not be doubted. Doubt, paradoxically, became the proof of existence.

His approach is highly relevant to the workplace today. It invites us to see doubt as:

- A discipline and process, not just a swirling feeling.

- A tool to challenge false certainties, much like medicine rules out false positives.

- A catalyst for clearer thinking.

Descartes' challenge still stands: 'It is not enough to have a good mind; the main thing is to use it well.'[7] How can doubt help us to use our minds constructively to lead and deliver wisely?

For leaders, the challenge is applying clear thinking to the messy realities of work. This is where Simone de Beauvoir's insights into doubt and ethics come in. She argues in *The Ethics of Ambiguity* (1947) doubt sharpens our ethical compass. 'Ethics is the triumph of freedom over facticity.'[8] In the workplace, this might mean having the courage to voice concerns about a decision that feels wrong, even if it risks disapproval. Ethics often feels like a big, abstract word, but in reality it lives in the small, everyday moments when doubt arises and we find the courage to speak up.

In leadership and coaching, this ethical dimension of doubt becomes especially tangible. As an executive coach, I am constantly alert to ethical tensions, especially because the agreement is a three-way relationship between the organization, the coachee, and myself. Without boundaries, it is easy to become entangled in an ethical dilemma. For example, when an organization asks me to deliver difficult feedback to a coachee that it has not been willing to share directly. The coach must never become the voice of the organization; doing so undermines safety, and safety is essential for meaningful change.

As our lives become more entangled with artificial intelligence, climate crisis, political uncertainty, and the demands of modern work, our ability to ask, 'are we doing the right thing?' is more important than ever.

The arts: doubt as a creative fuel

The arts are a rich seam of doubt. The British artist Dame Tracey Emin doesn't let doubt paralyze her; instead, it becomes her work. Whether it is an unmade bed, or neon declarations of vulnerability, she puts it out there – sharing her inner world: thoughts, disappointments, desires, and shame. Recently, as she has faced into the most challenging of illnesses, she hasn't hidden away. Instead, she has continued to share through her art.

Her most recent and acclaimed exhibition, *I followed you to the end*, was raw, painful, and intensely honest. Nothing was spared, and we, the viewers, are richer for it. At the same time, she has been focusing on her long-term legacy beyond her art: mentoring and sponsoring young artists and contributing to her local community in Margate.

As Emin shows, doubt is a vital fuel for creators. I draw on many examples throughout this book to explore what the business world can learn from artists and their doubts – from David Bowie to the architect Frank Gehry and many more. Creatives understand the untapped power of doubt.

In my coaching work, people often tell me they are not creative. But we are all creators; whether finding a new way to present something, rethinking a problem, or finding a better way to connect with challenging stakeholders. So, the question is: *how can you give doubt a seat at the table to spark your creativity?*

Doubt remains one of the most underused forces in organizational life. If we can welcome it into the lab, onto the canvas and page – why not into the boardroom too? We need to build the muscle to do this well. In this chapter, we have explored what we can learn from other disciplines. In Part 2, on self-doubt, we will turn inward and look at what we can learn from ourselves.

Doubt distilled: a neglected discipline

- *Doubt lives in the space between.* Etymologically, *doubt* means to be caught between two. This duality is its power – it offers hesitation not as weakness but as pause for reflection. Embracing this tension enables better, more thoughtful leadership.

- *Doubt reveals what makes us distinct.* When we doubt parts of ourselves – faith, background, belonging – we often uncover unexpected strengths that organizations need more of, not less.

- *Other disciplines embrace doubt – why not leadership?*

  o *Science*: uses doubt systematically (experiments, peer review, falsifiability) to strengthen knowledge.

  o *Philosophy*: positions doubt as the starting point for clarity (Descartes) and moral courage (de Beauvoir).

  o *The arts*: creators like Emin and Bowie use doubt to provoke, disrupt, and produce their best work.

> *Doubt deserves a seat at the table.* In the workplace, doubt can feel taboo. But across disciplines, it is treated as a sign of thoughtfulness, creativity, and humility. When organizations legitimize doubt – making space for questioning, ambiguity, and challenge – they create conditions for better, braver outcomes.

It's time to ask: if doubt drives progress in science, philosophy, and the arts, why shouldn't it power creativity and clarity in business too?

Chapter 3:
The 'do' in doubt: Active Doubt

The opportunity in doubt is real, but doubt without action is tiring, rudderless, and unproductive. No board wants to see that in its leaders. No surprise, then, that most leaders steer clear. These are not the qualities that anyone wants to embody, let alone reward others in.

Leadership theory steers clear of it too. Doubt is the antithesis of how leadership is currently defined – vision, decisiveness, confidence, and followship. And yet in my own experience, doubt is present in almost every leader I work with. Rumbling quietly away underneath the surface. Present but not present. It reminds me of that cartoon which has two images of leadership side-by-side – one showing what we think leadership looks like, with a stick person triumphantly on top of a mountain, conquering and surveying all; and the other showing what leadership feels like, showing our stick person in a tangled mess. What if doubt could help untangle some of that mess? What if it is not what holds us back, but what helps us conquer the mountain?

The issue is not doubt itself.

It is our failure to make it useful.

We have built leadership models that leave out doubt, not because it lacks value, but because we have not yet given it a clear purpose. That is what this chapter is about: uncovering the 'do' hidden in *do*ubt – *Active Doubt*. Active Doubt is the bridge between introspection and movement forward.

Active Doubt is doubt with a constructive role. One that is increasingly vital as leadership evolves from the *chief* to the *chief collaborator*, a shift from the all-knowing authority to the leader who works through complexity alongside others.

Gallup, the global analytics and advisory firm, asked people in 52 countries what they most need from their leaders in its 2025 Leadership Report.[1] The number one answer was hope. Not trust, compassion, or stability – though those matter too – but hope.

Hope, however, does not stand alone. It is the companion of Active Doubt. Doubt challenges what is no longer serving us, what is no longer fit for purpose, and asks: *what could be better?* Hope is the belief that we can find that better.

You cannot lead with hope without doubt. Doubt without hope is paralysis. Hope without doubt is fantasy. Together, they create progress.

To work with doubt well, we need a new model – one that gives it a language, purpose, and structure to ensure it has a valid role in leadership today. The doubt-in- action model does exactly that. It sets out *why* we need doubt, through the lens of the forgotten discipline; *where* doubt happens, by naming Professional Doubt; *what* form it takes – self-, situational, and systemic doubt; *how* to engage with it, through the practice of Active Doubt; and the *outcome* it can create – brilliant doubt.

The doubt-in-action model

This is a map to direct your doubts, to get to a brilliant outcome. Without language, we cannot make sense of what we are experiencing nor share it with others. The doubt-in-action model provides this, and allows us to activate our doubts for good.

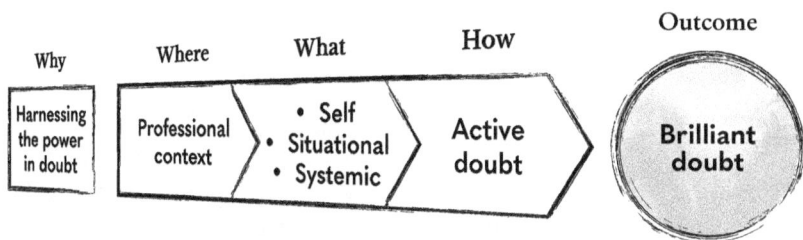

Figure 3: Doubt-in-action model

Professional Doubt: what psychologists can teach us about doubt

Professional Doubt describes how doubt shows up in leadership, work, and systems. It gives it a legitimate role.

In psychology it already has a professional role. It is the process that psychologists use in supervision. With their supervisor, the psychologist explores how they are working with individual clients and unpacks what they are missing. The British Psychological Society states that the ideal therapist doubts their professional skills – doubt is critical to them being effective. Research by Helene Nissen-Lie et al. supports this. She found that therapists who demonstrated a combination of professional self-doubt and personal self-compassion achieved better client outcomes than those that didn't. This combination 'seems to pave the way for an open, self-reflective stance that allows psychotherapists to respect the complexity of their work, and, when needed, to correct the therapeutic course in order to help clients more effectively with their challenges.'[2]

This frames Professional Doubt as a vital skill for effectiveness at work. There is no such thing as a new idea, but if we are going to borrow, then is there anyone better when talking about doubt than the experts of the mind?

Professional Doubt is also a mindset – a professional mindset.

When we are professional:

- We partner. We collaborate with doubt.

- We do not judge, nor shame. We are open and curious.

- We do not throw doubt in like a hand grenade and walk away. We stay with it. We work with it.

- We are committed to our development and to acquiring skills, including the skill of Active Doubt.

Having named the space doubt occupies professionally, let's turn to the form is takes, helping us to know what we are looking for and working with.

Professional Doubt: the three forms of doubt

In a professional context, doubt is much broader than our own internal feelings and reflects the interconnectedness of the system that we operate in. Situational and systemic doubts are the doubts that reside *outside* the person.

Type	The focus	What it is	The pattern
Self-doubt	Internal – inside self	Self-doubt relates to oneself and the doubts we are thinking and feeling about ourselves, perhaps questioning our ability or self-worth. Imposter syndrome is a form of this. It can be both short-term and pervasive. The benefit: it can mature the individual.	'I doubt I can do this.'

Type	The focus	What it is	The pattern
Situational doubt	External – outside self	Situational doubt is the form of Professional Doubt that is triggered by a *specific* event or context – a changing environment, unclear data, evolving relationships, or complex decisions. It is doubt you can point to and name. Often short-term and immediate – rooted in what is happening here and now. The benefit: it can mature the team and ultimately the organization.	*Contextual doubt*: 'I am doubting the relevance of this project, now we have the new strategy in place.' *Data doubt*: 'The numbers don't correlate with the feedback we have had.' *Relational doubt*: 'I don't trust this person to support me with the management team.' *Decision-making doubt*: 'I don't know whether we should choose to hire person A or B for this role.'

Type	The focus	What it is	The pattern
Systemic doubt	External – outside self	The unease or questioning that arises not from a person or event, but from the wider structures, norms, or environment. It comes from the system itself – its values, behaviours, power structures, and the invisible architecture that shapes what is seen, said, and done. Systemic doubt's source can be multilayered and interconnected. Often long-term and structural. The benefit: it can mature the system.	'What in the system is not allowing junior people to be able to raise their concerns in an organization?'

When we think about doubt, we often focus on self-doubt, the doubt we are most consciously familiar with. For many of us it is a daily presence in our lives – a shadow to our thoughts. We do not always acknowledge or give space to the role of situational and systemic doubt in how we lead, and how we generate results. Actively expanding our consciousness of doubt in all its forms will help us lead more effectively, by being open and compassionate with ourselves, in turn creating space for doubts to be aired in the team, and in the wider organization.

These three forms of Professional Doubt are interconnected; the doubt of one can cast a shadow and/or light on the others. We can doubt our capability (self-doubt), which may be exacerbated by concerns about the amount of resource we have available to deliver the project (situational doubt), which is then compounded by a culture where truth to power is not spoken without consequence (systemic doubt). Likewise, systemic doubt can trigger concerns in ourselves: if the structures in place do not make it easy for people like us to do well here, we may start questioning whether we are enough.

We see these three forms of doubt vividly in the film *Conclave* (2024), based on Robert Harris' novel. Cardinal Lawrence, played by Ralph Fiennes, struggles with self-doubt ('I lack the spiritual depth to be Pope'), while also facing situational doubt when a new cardinal unexpectedly arrives, raising questions about secrecy and hidden motives. Beneath it all runs systemic doubt: unease about the Church's power structures and the dangers of certainty. As Lawrence puts it,

> *'Certainty is the great enemy of unity... If there was only certainty and no doubt, there would be no mystery, and therefore no need for faith.'*

The benefit of labelling doubt

By categorizing and naming the different forms of doubt, we acknowledge their presence, opening up the possibility of using specific strategies to leverage each form. Naming is used extensively in Cognitive Behavioural Therapy – if you can name it, you can tame it. For example, 'my doubts are coming from the mistrust between myself and my colleague'. It is the start of trying to catch it; you can't catch something you cannot see. It stops it feeling overwhelming, allowing you to examine it and move forward. It stops generalizations and 'all or nothing thinking' – 'I am terrible at all sports' vs. 'I am a good runner, but I find racket sports hard.' By being specific we can start to move into action.

Imagine you are a newly promoted member of the Executive Leadership Team. At your first meeting, everyone agrees with a recommendation to acquire a new business, creating synergies and opening a new route to market. But something doesn't sit quite right with you. Maybe it's instinct, or maybe it's that you weren't convinced by the merging businesses' response about their future product pipeline plans.

You speak up, but only vaguely: 'I'm not sure about this.' Colleagues downplay it, and the conversation quickly moves on. What you didn't do was name your doubt clearly: 'I'm concerned the product pipeline is too weak to justify the price.' Without naming it, the doubt had no weight.

Once the business is acquired, it becomes clear that the innovation pipeline is not sufficient. Your doubt had been right, but it wasn't voiced with enough clarity or conviction to challenge others.

The hidden benefit of doubt is that it matures the person, the situation, and the system. This begins with our relationship to self-doubt. When we are present to our internal doubts, we can examine them objectively and build a healthier relationship with them – asking: how can this help me grow beyond my comfort zone? We take what is useful and leave what is limiting.

A healthy relationship with self-doubt also gives us the courage to voice situational and systemic doubts. Doubting a situation or system can be a valuable challenge to the status quo, but only if we trust our doubts enough to name them. Otherwise, we dismiss them, rarely pausing to ask: what's really going on here? What is trying to emerge? By sitting alongside our doubts, we strengthen our ability to speak them into the wider world.

When a situation welcomes doubt, it creates space for new thinking and new paths forward. When a system welcomes doubt, it recognizes that it can only evolve with its help. Evolution requires doubt. Over time, working with doubt shapes maturity and steadiness in leadership, offering the wisdom of the elder that strengthens the self, the situation, and the wider system.

Naming our doubts is the first step. To mature them, we must work with them and move towards resolution. That is Active Doubt.

Rolling our sleeves up: Active Doubt

On its own, naming doubt changes little. Doubt must be active.

When doubt rolls up its sleeves, you can look it squarely in the eye and ask what it needs to reach a good outcome, whether that's a new insight, a reframing of the situation, or a clear decision. *Doubt is a tool to help decide.* When doubt is not active it becomes inactive; this is the doubt we are perhaps most familiar with.

Active Doubt
- Asks questions with purpose
- Shares concerns
- Seeks diverse perspectives
- Learns from what doubt reveals
- Moves with energy and curiosity
- Informs decisions thoughtfully

Inactive Doubt
- Ruminates without direction
- Stays silent or hesitant
- Stays isolated on one view
- Ignores what the doubt is telling it
- Feels heavy or draining
- Swirls in indecision

Figure 4: Active vs Inactive Doubt

Notice whether you occupy Active Doubt or inactive doubt more often, and ask: what would help you to move into the Active Doubt space?

In the self, situational, and systemic parts of this book, I will take you through how you can use Active Doubt to get the outcome you want: practical and actionable support.

Putting Active Doubt to work

I coached the CEO of a fast-scaling tech business. Where he excelled was rolling his sleeves up sitting with a whiteboard and his team, working through challenges together. He had a bias towards action, coming alive when he was immersed working

Active Doubt is doubt with its sleeves rolled up.

through the issues, challenges, and doubts to find the solutions. The doubts were the drivers to move into action:

- Who can I ask for feedback on my performance?

- Whose voice have we not heard in this meeting?

- Who can play the role of doubt in this meeting?

Taking inspiration from this questioning approach, in each of the following sections on self-, situational, and systemic doubt, we explore practical ways to make doubt active.

One of the clearest examples I've seen of Active Doubt in action came from Lydia, a Head of Delivery known for driving bold change. Her doubt didn't paralyze her – it prompted a rethink. Not of her value, but of her role.

Brilliant doubter: Lydia, Head of Delivery

Before I tell you about Lydia's doubts, you need to know she is brilliant at her job – able to galvanize an often-reluctant organization into action, building genuine relationships from the top to the bottom. Yet she has moments of deep self-doubt. It's not evident on the outside; she swears like a trooper, holds her own in meetings, and whips the organization into making change. If I wanted something to happen, I would want Lydia by my side.

In one of her coaching sessions, she described how she had recently recruited three new direct reports – great hires, older than her, and with more functional experience. Her doubts were kicking in: would they rate her, knowing they had more technical expertise? How could she possibly add value?

She spoke at speed, packing the air with words – as if her swirling, doubtful mind had taken form right in front of me.

It all slowed down, quickly, with one question: what was the advantage of her leading the team without the same level of technical knowledge as them? This shifted her into thinking about how she was going to redefine her role now with this expanded team. Identifying that her focus was different now and focused on delivering the strategy and managing key stakeholders.

Her breathing slowed, the animation lessened, and the self-doubt had served its purpose: to motivate her into action to redefine her role.

Discovery questions

Lydia was being triggered by both her new role and her new colleagues (a relational trigger). Her example highlights that there are times when it can be an advantage to have less experience or skill in a certain area.

- Can you recall a time when inexperience was a benefit for you?

- What, if any, is the advantage of you having less experience or skill in the area you are doubting? How might this help you approach the work differently or create space for others?

- What is your role now, and how does it differ from what you have done before? What might need redefining now that your responsibilities, team, and context have changed?

- What assumptions are you making about what others expect of you? Which are real, perhaps based on a conversation, and which are your own thoughts?

- How might your doubt be encouraging you to grow here?

Overview of the doubt-in-action model

Concept	Function	Description
Doubt, the forgotten discipline	Why	Doubt has long been central to disciplines like science, art, and philosophy, where it is used to making thinking and outcomes better. And yet in organizations we neglect this discipline of doubt, as we try to move towards certainty in this volatile world.
Professional Doubt	Where	Professional Doubt is the umbrella term for the three forms of doubt we experience in organizations. To benefit from it, we need to engage with it professionally and deliberately because when ignored, it no longer serves us.
Self-, situational and systemic doubt	What	Professional Doubt takes three main forms: 1. *Self-doubt:* internal doubts arising from our own narratives and insecurities. Includes imposter syndrome. 2. *Situational doubt:* external doubts arising from situations. 3. *Systemic doubt:* external doubts arising from the wider system.
Active Doubt	How	The practice of Professional Doubt and how we engage with doubt to move forward constructively and not become paralyzed.

Concept	Function	Description
Brilliant doubt	Outcome	The benefit of using doubt constructively. A leadership and organizational superpower in times of complexity and change.

Professional Doubt is the umbrella for all forms of doubt we experience at work. Active Doubt is what happens when we channel it into something useful.

Consider:

- Where in your work right now would it be useful to pause and question an assumption you've been treating as fact?

- Who might benefit if you voiced the doubt you've been holding privately?

- How might your leadership look different if you treated doubt as data, not weakness?

Doubt distilled: doubt getting active

- *Doubt isn't a weakness – it's a signal.* When engaged with purpose, doubt helps us see what's really going on beneath the surface.

- *Professional Doubt gives doubt a place.* It legitimizes doubt in leadership, work, and systems – not as personal failure, but as professional wisdom.

- *There are three faces of Professional Doubt: self, situational, and systemic.* Each type points to different sources of uncertainty – and each invites its own kind of response.

- *Self-doubt shapes how we voice other doubts.* Our relationship with our own inner doubt impacts our ability to challenge situations and systems.

- *Active Doubt is doubt with its sleeves rolled up.* It doesn't just question – it listens, learns, and helps move things forward.

- *Inactive doubt gets stuck.* It isolates, ruminates, or avoids – leaving insight and possibility on the table.

- *Brilliant doubters are courageous collaborators.* They partner with doubt, stay with discomfort, and use it to generate clarity and action.

- *To 'do' doubt is to lead wisely.* In a complex world, certainty is fragile – but doubt, well-handled, is a tool for truth, progress, and trust.

What might become possible if I actively changed the way I relate to my own self-doubts?

'The test of a first-rate intelligence is the ability to hold two opposed ideas in mind at the same time and still retain the ability to function.'

- F. Scott Fitzgerald

part two

Self-Doubt

Chapter 4:
The doubtful self I: what shapes us

Our self-doubt is shaped by our inner thoughts and beliefs, and can be rudely awakened by external triggers. Of course, some doubts are unhelpful, which is why it matters to understand where they come from – doubt is neither all good nor all bad.

In Matthew Haig's novel *The Midnight Library*,[1] he writes about Nora Seed, a woman who is overwhelmed by regrets and considering ending her life. She finds herself in an alternate reality, a place called the Midnight Library. A library filled with stories of the many lives she could have lived had she made different choices – wild and varied possibilities. A library of hope, showing her how to move forward with her own life.

Whilst the Midnight Library is fiction, we all walk around with enormous libraries in our heads; stories we read about ourselves and share with others, shaped by our past experiences, beliefs, and values. Stories that influence how we show up and our self-doubts. A library that sometimes serves us and sometimes is out of date. Perhaps there is a new version, but we have forgotten to read that copy of the book. Instead, the old version is still on automatic replay in our head.

Doubt becomes wired in to our way of thinking about ourselves. At the gnarly roots of our self-doubt are broad sweeping beliefs relating to our identity and how we see ourselves. These roots wrap around our often-fragile confidence:

- 'I am not clever enough' – the belief that one's intelligence is insufficient.

- 'I don't deserve success' – an underlying feeling of unworthiness.

- 'I am not lovable' – the belief that we cannot be loved.

- 'I am too loud / scary / quiet' – the fear that one is unacceptable as one is.

- 'I am not enough' – the belief that one's intrinsic value is lacking.

As we can see, doubt often stems from the deeper fear that we are not enough. However, Marianne Williamson challenges this perfectly when she writes:

> 'Our deepest fear is not that we are inadequate. Our deepest fear is that we are powerful beyond measure. It is our light, not our darkness that most frightens us. We ask ourselves, "Who am I to be brilliant, gorgeous, talented, fabulous?" Actually, who are you not to be?'[2]

These beliefs stem from our experiences, values, and personality, which together shape our identity.

Experiences: the echoes from our past

A client described how she had sailed through school, her intelligence a reliable anchor for her internal narrative, mirrored in her external world when she was always top of her class. She went to university and it changed. She was with people of similar intelligence and had to work hard to keep her middle rankings in class. It was not a position she was familiar with, and a new feeling of self-doubt emerged as she questioned her ability for the first time. This formative experience shaped her identity and challenged how she saw herself.

As she navigated her career and found herself in new situations, the old story from that difficult time re-emerged. It ran silently in the background, linking yesterday's emotions with her present experiences of starting a new role or going for an interview, firing up her self-doubt again. These echoes of the past turn isolated incidents into patterns, colouring how we react in the present.

Our past experiences press replay on the script in our head, and when it looks like a new script is playing, it can simply be a remake of the old version. It is not only negative experiences that drive doubt. Positive ones can take over the driving seat. Someone who has grown up receiving lots of praise from parents and teachers can find their self-doubt triggered when they are working in a more autonomous working environment, where there is not a culture of continual positive feedback. This leads them to question if they are measuring up to others' expectations and standards, when faced with a stone wall of silence.

* How might your past experiences be showing up in your present self-doubt?

* What is the silent script that runs your self-doubt?

These scripts are part of the stories we tell ourselves and we will explore what we can do with them in Chapter 7 – the 'do' in self-doubt.

Finding out my client's internal stories is key. Often, we need a new story or, as I think about it, a software update. Sara was due her software update:

Brilliant doubter: Sara, Finance Director

The Greek god Atlas was burdened by the heavens weighing down on his shoulders. Sara, in her coaching session, likened her experience to the same burden. Now, whilst Atlas was burdened, he was also one of the strongest Greek gods – and Sara is strong. She had weathered much in her personal life and professionally navigated choppy waters full of corporate pirates. The good news: the safety of the shore was in sight; there were only two months before she would leave. She had even processed the anger generated by the pirates. Yet, she felt burdened. Happy and relieved to leave… but still burdened.

This metaphorical burden on her shoulders was her self-doubt. We explored it and it led to a true mic drop moment – the kind that gives you a dopamine high because the shift is so immediate and profound for the person. The dopamine rush came from one simple question:

'What is your doubt about?'

Silence.

A simple reply followed. 'Actually… I don't have doubt.'

Mic dropped, and with it the doubt. What had changed? She realized her doubt was a habit – an old story that she was rereading. When she had been silent, she had mentally been going through her list of doubts – doubt about her ability to do the job, lead her team, work collaboratively with colleagues, and deal with the pirates that lurk in every organization. However, there were concrete facts that demonstrated her abilities in these areas. Her department had been audited, and no issues had been found; instead, there was a complimentary report praising her work. Her team loved her, evidenced by their comments at the recent Christmas party. She had a strong internal network, and as for the pirates, she had learnt a new set of skills to manage them.

She decided there and then to leave her book of doubt on her desk. It was no longer needed. Sara's example is a reminder that not all doubts are worth keeping. Some are habits: old stories we carry long after the evidence has proved them false. Those doubts need to be challenged, even discarded. But others are different: they are signals, drawing our attention to something we might otherwise miss. These are the doubts to harness. The art of brilliant doubt lies in knowing the difference.

Discovery questions

Could your doubt be a habit? It is a powerful insight, just as Sara realized. She crushed her habit when she realized it was a book of fiction. We need to check in with our thinking and see how much of it is a habit that no longer serves us, or whether it has evolved and needs updating.

- What stories do you use to reinforce your doubts? Are these still up to date?

- Is this a new doubt or a familiar one wearing a new outfit?

- What concrete evidence challenges this doubt?

- What facts have you forgotten or dismissed?

- How could this doubt be a signal – not a stop sign?

Values: our inner compass

Our values are our inner compass, guiding how we show up, our interactions, and what we see as 'right'. When 'life' misaligns with our compass, it can jar abruptly, challenging our perceptions, creating conflict and doubt.

I worked with a leader who began to question whether she was in the right organization. The culture was fast-paced and demanding, and she believed deeply that work should enable people with families to thrive. When a manager questioned a colleague's decision to take time off during a busy period, she saw it as evidence that the organization's values were being compromised. It triggered deep doubt about whether her own principles could hold in that environment.

When we unpacked the story, the situation proved to be more nuanced. The manager's concern was logistical, not personal, and the colleague did in fact take the time off as planned. Her doubt was real, but it was driven by interpretation rather than fact. By exploring it, she realized her values weren't under threat — and that her doubt was highlighting a need for clarity, not confirmation of misalignment.

This is the power of values in shaping doubt. When our compass senses misalignment, we pause, examine, and test our assumptions. Sometimes the doubt confirms that something really is off-course. Other times, it clears the fog and helps us see things as they are. Either way, doubt sharpens our clarity.

What wakes the doubtful self?

Our doubtful self is woken up by external triggers, which can stem from the context, people, and situation. These can stir internal loops that create or intensify self-doubt. For example, someone might feel confident in one role but doubt themselves deeply after a promotion – not because they've changed, but because the situation has. Understanding and naming what is causing our doubt drives awareness and conveniently helps us to 'starrt' taking some action as a result of the doubt.

There are six triggers – S.T.A.R.R.T – for us to be aware of. These are:

Standards-related:	'I am not able to do the work to the standard that I want' or 'I cannot do this as well as others'.
Task-related:	'I am worried about whether I can present effectively to the senior leadership team next week'.
Ambition-related:	'I don't have enough experience to go for the promotion'.
Role-related:	'I don't think I have the ability to make the impact that I need to'.
Relational-related:	'I don't think my colleague respects me, as I am struggling to build a good relationship with them'.
Transition-related:	'I am worried that I am not going to be able to deliver the changes required in the new organization'.

This doubtful person (me) worked for Mars Confectionery. At the time, each person's position in the company was defined by what Zone they were. This classification system took on a life of its own. I was struggling to get to the 'lofty' status of a Zone 6 – in my head you had made it when you were a Zone 6. I never made it and left.

At Nokia I found myself in the opposite scenario – I kept getting promoted, every year. I believed my promotions were due to the yearly restructurings that happened – that I was 'lucky' to be in the right place at the right time. In my final role, I honestly believed the only reason I got it was because no one else was available. There were 'only' 125,000 people working for Nokia globally and I was the only one available? Skewed thinking. My doubtful self was highly critical and becoming louder with every promotion. I didn't believe I had earned them, especially as a once-failed Zone 6.

Self-doubt is the doubt in oneself, one's abilities, or one's judgment, and in the case of professional self-doubt, it relates to one's doubts, abilities or judgment in a work environment. In hindsight it gave me an unexpected gift. At Nokia I was given a coach to help me to develop my leadership style. This provided a window into my future career. Now I can't imagine doing anything else. My initial self-doubt paved the way to something better.

As I've seen in my own story – and in many of my clients' – doubt doesn't disappear with success. It evolves, shows up in different guises, and waits for familiar triggers. But once we know how to listen to it, we begin to change the script.

Doubt distilled: why it gets triggered

- *Doubt is a memory in disguise.* It often replays old stories, shaped by experiences that felt formative or defining at the time – even if they no longer reflect who we are now.

- *It's rooted in perception, not always in fact.* We carry narratives that were once useful, but may now be outdated or distorted by comparison, fear, or values misalignment.

- *Self-doubt doesn't vanish with success – it shifts shape.* Triggers like standards, tasks, ambition, roles, relationships, and transitions wake it up. Once we learn to name these triggers, we can stop being ambushed by doubt and start putting it to work.

- *Awareness is the first rewrite.* By noticing what wakes our doubt, we create the space to edit the story – not erase it, but evolve it.

When the doubt is woken, how does it speak to us?

Chapter 5:
The doubtful self II: how it speaks to us

Everyone has a doubtful self

Self-doubt is universal. It believes in fairness and equality, turning up as an uninvited guest. Whether you are a CEO, Director, or starting in your first role, self-doubt lurks. It is usually hidden – masked by confidence and often without a voice. It does not disappear with seniority or success. It evolves, and keeps showing up doing its work. And yet when we unpack it, we can see how it also contributes to our success. The first step is accepting its presence and then reframing our relationship with it.

Brilliant doubter: Meera, CEO

Meera led a public sector organization with approximately 1,800 employees and a £170 million budget. In our initial conversation, she told me she was painfully silent when she was in meetings with other CEOs – her peers. In these usually male-dominated meetings, she was not contributing her ideas, believing the other CEOs knew more. She was full of self-doubt.

The doubts could have remained in her head, causing mischief and stress. Instead, she chose to tackle them through coaching. The feedback I gathered from her peers showed that without exception, they valued and appreciated her perspective, describing how she brought new and different insights to the table. No one mentioned that she was a new CEO. Their perception of her was in complete contrast to her own thinking. The feedback helped her see the mismatch between how she saw herself and how others saw her.

Discovery questions

Meera's self-doubt was shaped by her false perception of what others thought, and by her underplaying the value she brought to situations. Consider:

- What self-doubts do you have that are based on 'mind reading'? Brilliant you may be, but a mind reader you are not. Instead, how can you get some fact-based evidence to influence your current perceptions?

- What are the additional skills that doubt is encouraging you to develop? Use the doubt to humbly ask what additional skills you may want to learn.

What are the different voices of self-doubt?

The voice of the imposter

A form of self-doubt is the imposter, often described as imposter syndrome. The imposter has a large presence in my work and many of my clients at some point acknowledge its presence. For many it is how self-doubt manifests in a professional context – 'I suffer from imposter syndrome.'

I was approached by someone who wanted to potentially do some coaching. In our chemistry call she told me: 'I have worked in marketing for ten years and risen quickly to a senior leadership position, thanks to an instinct for strategic thinking and problem solving, persuasive executive presence, and "right-place-right-time" factors that put me in senior roles of startups that quickly grew through M&A.'

Brilliant. She went on: 'I feel constantly out of my depth as a marketer. Others at my peer level have spent 20+ years earning their stripes, learning through experience, and observing how marketing works in other organizations or how other more senior marketers work. I've skipped a lot of this and have learned principally through experimentation and "doing." Now I feel rudderless.'

She spoke about what being 'rudderless' meant for her. She was able to develop strategies that people bought into, but she didn't know if the strategy was right. She worried she would get caught, and people would realize she didn't know what she was doing, especially as she had risen through the ranks so quickly.

She kept referring to 'the truth' – what if the truth was that she didn't know what she was talking about? She was surrounded (in her words) by 'good but flawed people,' and rather than thinking that everyone is flawed in some way, it made her worry that they were not asking the right things of her. Here was someone clearly doing well, and yet the imposter had taken up residency in her head.

The concept of the imposter was first identified by Pauline Rose Clance and Suzanne Imes over 45 years ago. Their paper, 'The Imposter Phenomenon in High Achieving Women: Dynamics and Therapeutic Intervention,'[1] explored the experience of successful women who attributed their success to external factors such as luck or other people rather than their own ability. They often felt like frauds who were waiting to be exposed as incompetent, despite clear evidence that their success was due to their own talents and efforts. In other words, their success was self-made. Note that this original research called it a 'phenomenon' and not a 'syndrome.'

The imposter lingers in the minds of those who experience it, working hard to keep its presence felt – through statements such as 'I am not enough,' 'I will be found out soon,' 'Others have more talent and have more right to be in this position than me.' They keep up a continual line of 'chat' to keep the person in their 'place.' According to the *International Journal of Behavioral Science*,[2] more than 70% of people experience this at some point in their lives. There are many imposters.

The imposter is not elitist. Most of us can relate to not feeling good enough, particularly in new roles or high-pressured environments or with others who speak highly of their own abilities.

There are four behaviours that people with an imposter can exhibit:

- *Procrastination*: the avoidance of the actual 'thing' so they don't have to face into the feelings. 'I will tidy my house first and then I will write the white paper which is due to be submitted at the end of the week.'

- *Perfectionism*: the crafting and detailing to ensure it is of the highest standard – they work, work, work to avoid it going wrong. 'I have spent most of this week writing the white paper and need to spend more time over the weekend to ensure that the argument is clear enough for the reader.'

- *People pleasing*: minimizing their needs and voice, giving power directly or indirectly to others. Saying 'yes' when 'no' would work better. 'Of course, I can include the input from the supply chain Director into the paper, it will be interesting to hear their perspective given that they have not worked on this project in the last two years.' In other words, they will add limited value and delay the writing of the paper even further.

- *Paralyzing silence*: staying quiet whilst others talk, even when they have ideas and thoughts that will add value to the discussion. The inner dialogue might be saying to the person, 'that is interesting what they are saying about the cause-and-effect correlation in the paper, I wonder if they have considered X, but then again maybe it is not relevant, and I haven't understood correctly. I will carry on listening to their points.'

The imposter often overstays its welcome, keeping up a constant inner dialogue. It avoids the facts and downplays our accomplishments, even when the proof is right in front of us. Imposter syndrome can often present itself when people are burning out through overwork or experiencing anxiety and depression – times when our internal narrative becomes disconnected from external reality.

Looking back at documents she'd written years earlier, my friend Yasmeen was surprised by how good they were. At the time, she hadn't believed they were any good – largely because her manager hadn't read them, which led her to question her own ability.

The voice of comparison

Self-doubt is often ignited and inflamed by comparison. Leon Festinger (1954), an American social psychologist, first identified the social comparison theory,[3] identifying that we often determine our own worth through comparison with others, and that we have an innate drive to evaluate ourselves against others to understand our own abilities and views.

As there are no easily accessible and universal standards by which to judge ourselves (in terms of intelligence, attractiveness, ability at work), we tend to make subjective judgments and rate ourselves against an arbitrary scale or viewpoint. Social media heightens the comparison trap, where we see carefully curated versions of each other's lives to tantalize and torment ourselves with. This skewed lens becomes the yardstick by which we measure ourselves, fuelling doubt and discontent.

Brilliant doubter: Sam, Head of HR

Sam's manager kept telling her, 'You could do my job' – a clear vote of confidence in her future as HR Director. But Sam didn't buy it. She saw her career growing sideways and had a persuasive story for why that made more sense. And yet, she was excelling. Her stakeholders rated her highly. The only problem was that she couldn't see what everyone else could.

She'd recently been asked to interview peers for senior roles and confessed to feeling threatened by them. They had conventional careers – steady progression through big organizations – a path very different from her own. Sam compared herself to them and found herself lacking. She also doubted her impact in meetings, worrying she didn't contribute enough. But when I asked whether she'd ever had that feedback, the answer was a firm no.

She was telling herself that she was just lucky, always in the right place at the right time. But as we unpacked it, her real strengths emerged: she built trust quickly, offered wise counsel, and was deeply valued by her senior stakeholders. She had earned her seat at the table – she just hadn't claimed it yet.

Sam is purpose-driven. She loves her organization and wants to make it one of the best places to work. She'd believed she could achieve that from her current role – but in our coaching, we explored the multiplier effect of leadership. If she truly wanted to deliver on her purpose, stepping up would give her the platform to do it. She left our session ready to say yes to a new responsibility – something she'd previously thought she wasn't ready for.

Comparison had distorted her self-perception – but once she reclaimed her own story, she could step into her next chapter with clarity and confidence.

Discovery questions

* Am I seeing the whole picture, or judging it against the highlight reel of someone else's life?

* What strengths do I bring that cannot be easily measured or compared?

* What, if anything, does this comparison have to teach me?

* What advice would I give someone else in my position?

* What would change if I stopped comparing myself to others?

The voice of ease

We often doubt ourselves when we fail to see our gifts and talents. When things come naturally and easily to us, we assume they are easy for others too. The ease makes us question and undervalue these talents, when in fact they are often our superpowers. This was first identified by Dr Valerie Young in her book *The Secret Thoughts of Successful Women* (2011)[4] and she called it 'natural genius'.

This is reinforced by the Dunning Kruger Effect, first described in 1999, which notes how people with a low ability in a particular area overestimate their competence, whilst those with a high ability tend to underestimate theirs. They found people who performed poorly on tasks (such as logical reasoning or grammar) consistently rated their performance as much higher than it actually was. Meanwhile, highly skilled individuals tended to assume that others had similar abilities, leading them to undervalue their expertise.

We often misjudge ourselves: the less we know the more confident we feel. The more we know, the more we doubt. Expertise can breed self-questioning. It shows that both overconfidence and 'over-doubt' can distort our reality and keep us from truly seeing ourselves and our talents.

Discovery questions

- Am I discounting my skills because they come naturally?

- What do others think are my greatest strengths?

- When others comment on my work, what comes up the most?

- How do I make things happen? How would other people describe how I make things happen?

- If someone else had my skills and experience, would I question their abilities the way I'm questioning my own? Or is this a self-imposed standard?

When it is not doubt: the voice of anxiety

Whilst we are focused on self-doubt, we also need to acknowledge that many people experience other challenges in the workplace. In *Atlas of the Heart*, Brené Brown opens with a powerful chapter titled 'Places We Go When Things Are Uncertain or Too Much,' where she identifies emotional states such as stress, overwhelm, worry, avoidance, excitement, dread, fear, vulnerability – and anxiety.[5]

Self-doubt tends to centre on internal beliefs about our competence or worth – it may manifest in thoughts like 'I am not good enough' or 'I can't build strong relationships at work.' In contrast, anxiety is rooted in concern about the future – 'I can't stop thinking about everything that might go wrong.'

Anxiety can take the form of persistent overthinking, physical symptoms like a racing heart, or feelings of isolation. With self-doubt, there is a duality to it – the challenge and the positive side which can prompt both reflection and growth. In contrast there is no duality to anxiety and it often needs deliberate intervention.

The cognitive biases behind the voices

The voices of doubt are how we experience it day to day. But underneath those voices lie powerful mental shortcuts – cognitive biases – that shape how doubt takes hold and keep it alive. We can become trapped by them. Cognitive biases are shortcuts the brain uses – they are helpful at times but they also fuel unnecessary doubt. Shining a light on them can help us understand the role they can play.

The fear bias: doubt is the handbrake of fear

One of the common cognitive patterns I see in my coaching is the invisible way fear quietly dresses up as self-doubt. Fear is the engine – it kicks in when we face uncertainty or risk. Doubt is the handbrake we instinctively pull to slow down or to stop to gain a sense of control.

Fear triggers our fight-or-flight system – a fast, unconscious response designed to keep us safe. But it's often too efficient, unable to distinguish between real and perceived danger. So, it shows up in everyday work moments: a big presentation, a new job, a stretch opportunity. We react as if we're under threat, even when we're simply being stretched.

Since we can't physically flee a meeting or fight the person giving tough feedback, the energy has to go somewhere. It often shows up as doubt. We pull the handbrake – hesitate, overthink, procrastinate. It gives us a sense of control, a way to limit risk.

But to grow in our working lives, we may need to release the handbrake. That doesn't mean eliminating fear – just choosing not to let doubt drive the whole vehicle. Doubt is a signal. A signal to tell us what's going on under the hood.

Discovery questions

- What fear or perceived risk might my self-doubt be trying to protect me from in this instance?

- Where have I felt this kind of doubt before, and what helped me then?

- If I were to release the handbrake, what is the worst that can happen?

- What if it went right?

- How might I take one small step forward – even with the handbrake partially on?

Availability bias

Availability bias is all about the recent, what is top of mind. It was identified by Amos Tversky and Daniel Kahneman (1973). They found that we rely on mental shortcuts to process the high volumes of information we are dealing with, by recalling examples. Practically, this means that things we have experienced recently, were particularly memorable, or that perhaps might have been emotionally striking, are etched more prominently in our minds.

Say a recent initiative failed and the fallout was public. When we are leading the next initiative, the recent memory might loom large, and we might doubt our capability, despite a track record of success. On the flip side, if things went well last time, we may skip the level of critical thinking (and doubt) that is still required to make it a success.

Discovery questions
To counter this, we need to pause and 'doubt our own thinking' by asking:

- What does the objective data actually tell me about this situation?

- Am I focusing on one vivid example? What are the counterexamples where it went well?

* Am I rushing to a conclusion? What time and information would help me make a more grounded decision on this?

* Am I treating this as an isolated situation? What are the broader patterns and themes happening here?

Confirmation bias

Confirmation bias is when we are filtering and processing based on what we want to see. It is how social media echo chambers thrive. If we already believe something is true then we tend to filter out data, facts, and ideas that would run counter to our thinking. For example, if we think we are not as capable as our colleagues, then we filter for evidence which confirms that, such as a colleague being praised for a presentation, or who, we learn, has an impressive education and exam results.

Discovery questions

We can 'doubt' our own (and others') confirmation bias by asking:

* What evidence would genuinely challenge my current belief?

* What assumptions am I making that could prove wrong?

* If this doesn't work out as I expect, what might my future self wish I had noticed sooner?

Doubt distilled: the voices of doubt

* *Doubt is universal.* It doesn't disappear with seniority or success – it just changes costume. Whether you're a new joiner or a CEO, doubt still finds a way in.

* *Doubt is often perception, not reality.* We frequently misread how others see us, underestimate our value, or assume we're not enough – even when the evidence says otherwise.

- *Doubt shows up in disguise.* It doesn't always call itself 'doubt.' It might arrive as procrastination, perfectionism, people-pleasing, silence – or that sinking feeling you're not qualified.

- *Comparison and self-narrative distort our view.* When we compare ourselves to others or cling to outdated stories about who we are, we forget our strengths – and shrink ourselves unnecessarily.

- *Fear fuels doubt – but doesn't have to steer.* Doubt is often a protective handbrake, pulled when fear kicks in. But recognizing the fear behind the doubt helps us choose how we respond.

- *Doubt can be a powerful coach.* If we get curious, doubt can point to what matters, highlight our growth edge, and push us towards greater clarity, courage, and impact.

What would change if you started treating your doubt as a leadership strength?

Chapter 6:
The brilliant leader: how doubt unlocks leadership power

Certainty is a velvet trap – comfortable and quietly paralyzing. We find comfort in the known: our habits, our skills, our past successes. But self-doubt offers something else – the hand of uncertainty. This may not make it compelling at first. Doubt rarely does. Most people wait for certainty before acting and, because certainty never arrives, they don't act. Self-doubt is not a signal to stop. It is a call to step forward, explore and, ultimately, escape, the velvet trap.

In this chapter, we will explore how doubt can become a doorway to strength and leadership.

The doorway of doubt

'Some of my greatest successes came from when I had the most doubt.'
—Clafoutie Sintive, Senior Innovation Director for
International, Glanbia

Doubt acts as a doorway – on one side is comfort, and on the other is growth. Doubt is a signal that we are leaving what is known to pursue what is possible. The doorway transports us towards our ambitions; our dreams and goals, where we want to be in the future. Brilliance does not exist on the safe side of that doorway. It lives beyond it. Brilliance requires doubt to succeed.

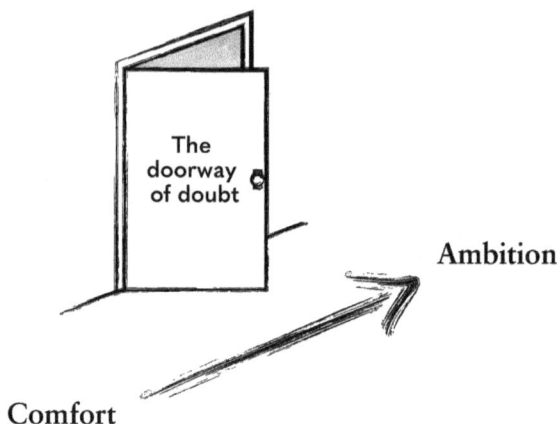

Figure 5: The doorway of doubt

If you were to stand at the doorway of doubt:

- What is on the other side of it for you?
- What is stopping you from walking through it?
- What or who do you need to help you cross?

To walk through the doorway requires courage, and a willingness to work in partnership with it. When we can see that doubt serves a purpose, we no longer need to fight it. By sitting comfortably with our doubts, we can access the superpowers they bring with them. These are:

- *The ambition spark* – doubt can be the signal that we're striving for more.
- *The trust builder* – we connect more deeply by sharing our concerns.

- *The critical thinker* – doubt enables us to question and challenge our thinking to get to better outcomes.

- *The creative power* – doubt can be the seed that helps us reimagine and innovate.

- *The collaborator* – doubt reminds us that we don't have to do it all ourselves, and that others strengthen us.

- *The coach* – doubt encourages us to ask, how can I be even better?

Let's explore each of these in more detail.

The ambition spark: doubt as a sign you are growing

Self-doubt can signal we are being stretched. A stretch towards ambition. On this subject Michelle Obama reflected:

> *'I still have a little imposter syndrome… it doesn't go away, that feeling that you shouldn't take me seriously. What do I know? I share that with you because we all have doubts in our abilities, about our power and what that power is.'*[1]

From the outside, you would never know. I saw her speak at London's O2 Arena, promoting her book. She could easily outsource her writing to a ghost writer, yet she does not. It is all her own hard-found words. I paid the equivalent of rock star prices to see her, and she more than delivered – intelligent and inspiring, funny and fearless. And yet here she is, telling the world that she still experiences imposter syndrome, despite all her achievements. One of the best examples of a brilliant doubter there is. If she can doubt and succeed, why can't the rest of us?

Her comments remind us: the imposter does not leave as we grow – it can keep up with us. Its presence tells us we are getting out of our comfort zone and pushing forward. What if we took its presence as a sign of achievement? The uninvited guest's gift is to highlight our growth.

Sometimes, doubt comes from within. Other times, it's handed to us – a challenge, a comment, an unexpected shift. But whether driven by fear of failure or a pull towards purpose, doubt has one thing in common: it shows we care.

For some leaders, doubt sounds like: 'I never want to feel that small again.' For others, it's: 'I need to step up – this mission matters.' Both are ambition, just in different voices.

The presence of doubt doesn't always mean 'I'm not enough.' Sometimes, it means 'I care enough to want more.' That shift in perspective is what transforms doubt from a weight into a source of leadership strength.

Discovery questions

- How can your doubt motivate you to achieve even more?

- If you had no doubt at all, how might that limit your ability to achieve your goal??

- When did you take a leap forward despite your doubts and it worked out for you?

For senior leaders, ambition can take on a heavier weight. It's no longer just about their own progression – it's about the people they lead, the livelihoods they protect, the culture they shape. Self-doubt at this level doesn't stem from inexperience, but from the burden of responsibility.

They may have already achieved many of their career goals, but with influence comes impact – and the stakes feel higher. What if I get it wrong? What if the business suffers? What if people lose their jobs because of my decision?

At this level, doubt is not a lack of ambition. It's ambition in its most accountable form.

The trust builder: leading with honest doubt

Doubt drives ambition, but it also shapes how we present ourselves. Many leaders feel pressure to appear certain – yet true authenticity comes from acknowledging self-doubt openly and embracing the growth mindset. The No Doubt leader presents with certainty, and never admits to 'I don't know'. Even if it is at odds with the uncertainty of the situation. There is a tidiness about them, which doesn't quite ring true. Who are they are behind the corporate façade?

People connect when they see the human behind the title, the person fully feeling their feelings, acknowledging their thoughts (including the doubts), and admitting when we are wrong or do not know the answer.

Authenticity acknowledges doubt.

I am a political podcast nerd, apparently in the top 3% of political podcast listeners in 2024. For the record, this makes me have serious doubts about myself. 'The Rest is Politics: USA' with Katty Kay and Anthony Scaramucci is a favourite. In part because of my love for Anthony Scaramucci, the Director of Communications who lasted only ten days of Donald Trump's first term. My friends tell me this is not 'normal'.

It took me a long time to realize why I connected with this talkative finance/crypto guy. Then it hit me: his honesty and openness about his personal flaws makes him more relatable, not less. In an interview published in *The Profile*,[2] Polina Pompliano recounts how Scaramucci stood in front of a crowd and talked about how he missed the birth of his son whilst attending a convention with Trump (Mrs Scaramucci, understandably, started filing for divorce proceedings). This does not cast him in great light, but as Polina explains: 'He clearly relishes sharing these stories because he understands a simple truth about the human condition: we connect with each other far more deeply over our failures than our successes.' I would extend this to: we connect far more over our doubts and fears than we do over our confidence. Our doubts, when shared, provide a connection point, because we are showing more of ourselves; not just the polished perfect image, but the human.

One vivid example of this came from my years at Nokia where I became an expert at 'being restructured.' We restructured globally nearly every year; chaos rippled through the organization as we waited for the music to stop to see where we were going to land. There were many lessons on how not to do this: from the relentlessly positive leader, who ignored the personal impact of these changes on the individual, to the 'fend-for-yourself' leader, who disappeared as soon as they knew they were no longer going to oversee you. However, those who showed up and shared the uncertainty of the experience connected with people.

The Trust Equation (developed by David Maister, Charles Green, and Robert Galford)[3] identifies trust as being built from four elements:

$$\text{Trustworthiness} = \frac{\text{Credibility} + \text{Reliability} + \text{Intimacy}}{\text{Self-orientation}}$$

Figure 6: The trust equation

- Credibility: do you know what you're talking about?

- Reliability: do you consistently follow through on commitments?

- Intimacy: can people confide in you and feel safe?

- Self-orientation: do you focus more on yourself or others? Lower self-orientation increases trust.

Credibility, on the surface, is about a person's knowledge, skills, and expertise; it doesn't imply 'I doubt.' However, it is also about honesty. Do we tell the truth, even when it's inconvenient? Do we admit when we don't know something? And are we consistent in our words and actions? There are two sides to how we convey our credibility: our expertise, and our ability to express our doubts. When leaders express their doubts in organizations it builds trust.

Reliability is about following through. In the context of doubt, it is not about always having the answers – it is about staying present in the face of uncertainty, following up even when you don't have the full picture. Doubt can shake trust, but reliability rebuilds it through consistent action.

Intimacy creates a safe space. If we can be appropriately open and honest, it allows others to be open and honest with us too, and to express their own self-doubts. 'Appropriately' is the key word: there is a balance to be struck between sharing and building confidence in your leadership versus 'oversharing' in your leadership.

Self-orientation is crucial. When leaders are caught in their own doubts, their focus can turn inward towards their own needs and anxieties, rather than outward to those they lead. I worked with a leader who felt strongly about voicing his doubts with his peers. He grew frustrated when they didn't seem to trust him in return. His style was assertive, even confrontational, and he believed openness meant saying whatever he thought. But if he had shifted his attention from not only what he needed to express but also to what others needed to hear – what were their doubts? – his doubt could have become a bridge rather than a barrier. The problem wasn't doubt, it was self-orientation.

Brilliant doubter: Pam Burton, ex-COO of Funding Circle, early employee of LOVEFiLM

'When I first started working, I quickly found myself managing eight to ten people – and I hated it. I nearly left the company. Later, with support from my coach, I set a big blue-sky goal: to enjoy managing people – something I couldn't imagine at the time.

'Coaching helped me see the root of the issue: self-doubt. As I became more aware of my own doubts, I started recognizing them in others – which helped me lead with more empathy. That openness gave my team permission to surface their doubts too.

'What shifted everything was when my coach said, "You're already doing the role – that tells me you're worthy of it." I realized I was ignoring the evidence: I'd been promoted into this role. I believe in data, and this was data. That helped me see that my empathy and intuition weren't weaknesses – they were leadership strengths.'

Discovery questions

- Which leaders do you trust the most? How do they voice their doubts?

- In what situations at work could you share your doubts more openly – and what impact might that have?

- What were the consequences when your words and actions were misaligned?

The critical thinker: doubt as a strategic strength

I regularly coach lawyers – they are, in many ways, the embodiment of brilliant doubters. While there may be exceptions, I have yet to find a lawyer who is not exemplary at doubting. The discipline of law actively trains them to challenge data, question assumptions, and turn arguments on their head – doubt is their craft.

Doubt, used well, sharpens critical thinking. It illuminates potential risks. When used wisely, it becomes a form of personal risk assessment.

One client was deep into a recruitment process and could not put her finger on what was driving her unease. When we explored it, she recognized that the leadership team mirrored a highly toxic team she had once worked in – an experience she had no desire to repeat. Her doubt was a warning to tread carefully. Doubt before you sign.

Research by Spiro (1987)[4] on cognitive flexibility showed that doubt triggers a shift towards considering multiple perspectives. This in turn enhances our adaptive problem-solving capacity. Doubt often arises when there is something at stake – status, reputation, security. But it also signals possibility: 'Taking this new role is a risk. It's at a lower level than my previous one, but it will give me experience in a different sector – one I believe has more future growth. In the long run, I hope it will pay off.' This kind of internal dialogue reflects someone thinking critically – not dismissing doubt, but using it to make sound judgments.

Research carried out by Saïd Business School[5] at Oxford University, based on 150 CEO interviews, found that 71% not only acknowledged experiencing doubt, but embraced it as a basis for better decisions. Robust questioning brings robust thinking, making better decisions.

Brilliant doubter: Clafoutie Sintive, Senior Innovation Director for International, Glanbia

'Doubt, for me, is linked to curiosity. When I oversaw the marketing for SlimFast, there was a lot of doubt about the product. I too doubted whether I could turn it around; after all, it's the brand of the 80s. However, what I found was that it was an amazing product, full of vitamins, minerals, and protein. If you took the brand name off it, it tested well with consumers, but we had to find a new way in. We ran an agency pitch to find new ideas; at the final stage we tested two ideas with consumers. The first agency idea was safer, less risk taking, and did well with consumers. The other agency idea was completely innovative and risk taking, but when we tested it, it bombed with the consumer. I asked them to rework the idea and decided to go with the agency who had originally bombed. The level of internal doubt was high; it meant I had to be robust in my argument and solid in the choices I was making. The idea I chose thought about the brand in a different way – which we needed. I had a lot more energy with this agency, but you just don't know. There is no certainty. The risk paid off, generating a significant double-digit increase as a direct result of the new campaign.'

Discovery questions

Clafoutie channels her doubt into curiosity. Instead of playing it safe, she embraces the discomfort of uncertainty, follows her intuition – and then doubles down to build the facts for her argument. Her intuition has been fine-tuned over the years to help her take the calculated risks required to make the big leaps.

Consider:

* What happens when I choose safety over instinct – or instinct over safety?

* What does doubt look like for me in moments of risk?

* Where might I be underestimating the power of my intuition?

* What could go wrong, and what will I do if it does?

* What don't I know? What would I do if I did know?

The creative challenger: doubt as innovation fuel

Nothing is certain in the realm of creativity – everything is up for reinvention. The most original thinkers know that the deep water of doubt is the space to find the new, different, and wonderful, even where there is discomfort.

> 'I think it's terribly dangerous for an artist to fulfil other people's expectations; they generally produce their worst work when they do that. If you feel safe in the area that you're working in, you're not working in the right area. Always go a little further into the water than you feel you're capable of being in... you are just about in the right place to do something exciting.'[6]

The Starman reminds us that *self-doubt can be the birthplace of our best work – a positive agitator* that does not accept the status quo. It nudges us to ask: *have I done the best I can? How can I make this even better?* It loosens the edges of our thinking and invites new thoughts to arrive.

'I always operate with a healthy insecurity,' reflected the architect Frank Gehry. Gehry has designed icons like the Guggenheim in Bilbao and the Dancing House in Prague. Reimagining how buildings can look, bringing his own distinctive approach to them.

Self-doubt can be the birthplace of our best work – a positive agitator

'For me, every day is a new thing. I approach each project with a new insecurity, almost like the first project I ever did. And I get the sweats. I go in and start working, I'm not sure where I'm going. If I knew where I was going, I wouldn't do it.'[7]

Bowie and Gehry are creatives in the traditional sense. But creativity is not reserved for artists and architects. It shows up in how we change the structure of a report, design an event differently, or identify new ways to bring in new customers. Doubt can be a creative springboard – an invitation to ask: what is possible? An invitation to keep testing, refining, and pushing ourselves.

As Rania Robinson, CEO of the creative agency Quiet Storm, puts it:

'If you want to come up with something new and groundbreaking or even start a business or come up with an original idea, you have to be comfortable with doubt because there'll be no benchmark.'[8]

Doubt does not have to stifle creativity – it can instead unlock it. As we embrace AI and walk further into a world of automation and machine learning, creativity is going to be where humans continue to add value, where (as yet) it cannot be handed over to the machine.

Discovery questions

- How has my self-doubt sparked creativity in the past?

- Can I recall a time when I was uncertain about an idea and it proved to be the most creative work I did?

- What is my self-doubt inviting me to reimagine, and how might I begin?

The collaborator: doubt invites others in

Leadership is lonely. The stakes are high and ultimately it is down to you to make the right decisions. But more heads will almost always get us to a better place. When we doubt, we are more likely to seek extra counsel, to create stronger solutions.

One of our brilliant doubters described the challenges of going into an unknown situation and how self-doubt crept in. When she first moved to Asia with a global fashion brand she created a network of other fashion leaders there, who were all dealing with the same macro-economic situation and the changing dynamic between China and Hong Kong. 'The network gave me the confidence to communicate back to the board about what was happening. We collaborated amongst ourselves about how we could remedy and problem-solve together in terms of the challenges that we were facing.'

Brilliant doubter: Tim Coolican, CEO Milk Makeup

When I interviewed Tim, he spoke candidly about the binary nature of success at the top: you're either seen as a success or a failure. As a CEO, you can build an exceptional culture and coach your people brilliantly – but, ultimately, it's the numbers that define your tenure. A great culture without commercial results often leads to a short-lived leadership role.

That reality brings pressure. Doubt naturally creeps in when the stakes are high and decisions carry weight. Tim shared the importance of giving yourself grace – a reminder that no one makes perfect decisions – and focusing instead on sustaining momentum. 'There are always decisions I can make,' he reflected.

For Tim, collaboration is one of the most effective tools to navigate doubt. He works with in-person collaborators, like a coach, to help him contextualize challenges and carve out space to reflect. He also draws on 'proxies' – trusted external perspectives or alternative sources of insight that offer clarity when self-doubt clouds his thinking.

He recalled preparing a major board presentation late on a Friday evening. One of his trusted advisors called to say,

'I don't think it's your best work – you've missed a crucial part of the story.' It was frustrating feedback to receive in the moment, but by inviting someone else into his thinking, Tim had created space to be challenged. In doing so, he had effectively harnessed his doubt – and, as a result, strengthened his message.

Discovery questions

Doubt brings humility. It encourages us to seek others' input – to bring diversity of thought; utilizing talents, whether it's the gift of foresight, creativity, or different lived experiences.

Consider:

- Who can we collaborate with to bring the benefit of doubt to our thinking?
- Who are the proxies who can inspire you?
- Where would creating a 'collaboration team' help you most, in your work and career aspirations?

The coach: the growth in not knowing

Self-doubt is an acknowledgment that we are not the finished article. An invitation to learn. Jean Piaget, a Swiss developmental psychologist, argued that learning happens when individuals experience a cognitive conflict between their current knowledge and new information. To break through this, the learner must examine the new information and see if it fits into existing thinking or modifies it altogether. Their doubt is the trigger for learning. In work, this can happen when the context changes. If the business we work for is acquired, we will need to rethink how we operate to align with the parent company.

I witnessed this when Fitbit was acquired by Google, which challenged the team to rethink what they knew about how to launch devices, with new insight gained from the data giants. Likewise, there was insight for Google to learn from the device experts on the nimbleness with which Fitbit operated. The sale of Fitbit brought new context. Context is everything: you can succeed once, but changing context requires us to apply our expertise in a different way, to morph and flex accordingly.

The good news: self-doubt doesn't hinder learning – it enables it. In fact, research by Bjork & Bjork on Desirable Difficulties[9] shows that introducing challenges and uncertainty into learning enhances long-term retention and deepens understanding. When people are nudged out of comfort and into confusion, they learn more effectively.

This echoes what many leaders experience: doubt can feel like discomfort, but it's often a sign that new growth is on the way. It's not a block to capability – it's a signal that capability is expanding. When we see our doubts as an opportunity to learn, this enables us to see our potential.

Discovery questions

- What is my doubt encouraging me to learn?
- What is the perceived gap between myself and my peers, and what would I need to learn to close that gap?
- If I knew it was possible to learn this new skill, what would it mean for my goals?
- What would I try to learn if I gave myself permission to start from scratch?

The gifts of the imposter: a misunderstood leadership strength

The imposter's arrival is often painted as a professional liability. But what if it's a sign of brilliance? Research shows there are positive outcomes resulting from it. MIT Sloan Assistant Professor Basima

Tewfik's research looked at the relationship between 'imposter thoughts' and interpersonal effectiveness at work. She says:

> 'It's a compensation story: If I think other people think I'm smarter [than I think I am], I might be worried that I'm not actually that smart, so I might turn my focus to something else – which is making other people think I'm great socially. People pick up on what I'm doing, and they say "Wow, she's a great person to work with, I really like interacting with her at work."'[10]

Tewfik tested this across four studies involving individuals working for an investment company, doctors in training with their patients, and people interviewing for a promotion. She found that people compensated for having these thoughts by unconsciously having what she calls an 'other-focused orientation.' She found that, 'They were more empathetic, they were better listeners, they asked better questions.'[11] When an individual does this at work, others are likely to respond in a positive way. Tewfik cites research that shows workers with low interpersonal effectiveness can cost, on average, between $420,000 and $62.4 million annually for companies. Despite struggling with imposter syndrome, those with imposter thoughts are actually saving the business money and have strengthened their interpersonal skills.

Adam Grant, an author, psychologist and professor at Wharton School of Business at University of Pennsylvania, found that imposters tend to be more motivated to learn as they want to work on themselves, and are open to new insights and collaborating with more people. In his interview with Reece Witherspoon, Witherspoon reflected, 'I'd rather be a learn it all than a know it all.' She discussed her own relationship with imposter syndrome and how she had confronted the feelings directly by walking straight into challenge. Early in her career, she auditioned relentlessly and absorbed rejection after rejection, learning to 'chase [her] talents' rather than chase every dream. Years later, preparing to play June Carter Cash in *Walk the Line* (2005), she spent seven months rehearsing and wanted to quit almost daily – yet the performance won her an Academy Award. For Witherspoon, confidence isn't the starting point, it's the result: 'You don't need confidence to pursue a challenging goal,' she reflected, 'you build confidence through pursuing challenging goals.'[12]

Brilliant doubter: Hannah, Technology Director

Hannah was part of a global leadership team that felt, in her words, like a 'boys' club' – full of military references and old-school attitudes. She found herself questioning her legitimacy at the table, particularly as some of her former line managers were now her peers.

As she explored her self-doubt, she began to claim her place with more confidence. Three key insights helped her quiet the imposter:

* *Rewriting the narrative.* She discovered she was holding onto an outdated story about herself. We gathered 360-degree feedback, and one comment stood out: 'Everyone believes in Hannah – except Hannah herself.' Her internal narrative was misaligned with how others saw her.

* *Redefining belonging.* While she initially experienced the group as an 'old boys' club,' she realized she didn't need to emulate their behaviours. Instead, she focused on how *she* wanted to show up – authentically and powerfully.

* *Creating a visual anchor.* Hannah began to visualize herself sitting confidently at the table – a mental image she returned to often as a grounding tool.

A couple of years later, Hannah reached out to share that she had just been promoted to a UK Executive role. She was still using her 'mental photo' – a visual key that helped her walk through the doorway of doubt.

Rania Robinson, CEO for Quiet Storm reflects:

> *'In my experience, the people who have the most self-doubt are the most competent, most brilliantly talented people. Often, failings come from overconfidence, and complacency comes from overconfidence.'*[13]

Active Doubt begins when we stop seeing doubt as a flaw and start using it as a feature. When we acknowledge both its challenge and its brilliance, it becomes one of the most powerful forces in our leadership – not something to silence, but something to work with.

Doubt distilled: leading with clarity, courage, and uncertainty

- *Doubt is a doorway, not a wall.* Doubt marks the moment we move from comfort to ambition. It invites us to cross into growth, innovation, and stretch – even when certainty hasn't yet arrived.

- *Doubt signals growth and ambition.* Whether driven by fear of failure or desire for purpose, doubt often shows we're striving for something more. It's a marker of movement – not inadequacy.

- *Doubt builds authentic trust.* When leaders admit what they don't know, they make space for others to show up honestly too. Doubt, when expressed with integrity, creates trust through vulnerability and shared humanity.

- *Doubt sharpens critical thinking.* Doubt encourages us to challenge assumptions, stress-test decisions and identify risk. It transforms into strategic thinking when used to illuminate blind spots and prompt better questions.

- *Doubt fuels creativity.* The discomfort of not knowing is the birthplace of invention. Great ideas often emerge from questioning what exists and daring to imagine something different.

- *Doubt invites collaboration and learning.* Doubt makes us more open – open to feedback, to others' ideas, to learning. It positions us as learners, not finished articles, and in doing so, deepens both connection and capability.

Where might your doubt be pointing you to lead more boldly?

Chapter 7:
The 'do' in self-doubt: how to FLOW through it

'To be liberated dive toward doubt with great eagerness given to being surprised or remain ossified a safe distance from alive.'
—Maria Popova[1]

Imagine the sea of doubt is warm and inviting – not something to avoid, but something to explore. With a little training – and a pair of armbands – we can learn to swim with it. This chapter is that training in how to let doubt carry you forward, rather than drag you under.

To be doubtful

'I am doubtful I will be promoted this year.' 'I am doubtful that I can build a strong working relationship with Mike as he is so different to me.' Or (as I type this), 'I am doubtful I will ever finish this book.' Doubtful literally means 'full of doubt' – and that fullness can weigh us down, as if we are going to sink to the bottom of the sea.

Psychologist Mihaly Csikszentmihalyi wanted to understand how people felt when they most enjoyed themselves and why. He called it 'flow' – 'a state in which people are so involved in an activity that nothing else seems to matter; the experience itself is so enjoyable that people will do it even at great cost, for the sheer sake of doing it.'[2]

This is the state I was aspiring to when I was marathon training, the state I am striving for as I type these words on the screen... that sweet spot that sometimes appears and sometimes doesn't. When we are in flow it is not because something is easy, like kicking back on a sun lounger with a good book. Whilst enjoyable, it would eventually lead to boredom. Instead, there is a correlation between the challenge and skill: if something is too small a challenge and you are highly skilled, it will lead to boredom; conversely, if it is too high a challenge and you don't have the skills, it leads to anxiety.

Csikszentmihalyi explains that

> 'the best moments usually occur when a person's body or mind is stretched to its limit in a voluntary effort to accomplish something difficult and worthwhile.'[3]

Exploring our doubt for meaning is the challenge and to understand it is worthwhile.

Moving from doubtful to doubtflow

Csikzentmihalyi points out how flow can improve people's lives. We often believe self-doubt kills momentum, but paradoxically it can create momentum if we choose to walk with it. Doubt is an invitation to think, refine, and discover the direction that matters – moving from doubtful to doubtflow. Flow helps us to find the wisdom in our doubts, to find the action to work through them.

Brilliant doubter: Yasmeen, Marketing Director

When Yasmeen left her last role, she found herself in the middle of both a personal and a market transition. 'You kind of attach your identity to a company,' she reflected, 'and after leaving, I was trying to work out who I was. I couldn't quite place myself. I kept thinking: what do I do now? Alongside this my confidence was low from the tough challenges in my last company.'

She had no plan for what came next until a friend suggested she start a podcast. That single nudge became a two-season podcast, a media partnership and a launch with a large advertising conference, with more planned to follow.

'I had never done a podcast before,' Yasmeen said. 'I started learning. I taught myself how to edit on YouTube, how to interview, how to tell stories in audio. I drew on my raw ingredients as a marketer – storytelling, creativity, making content – and applied them in a new form.

You can let doubt make you inactive – watching Netflix, waiting for the knock on the door, or you can use it as fuel. For me, leaning on friends, my network, and my own relentlessness helped me to move from that stuck place into action.'

Her doubt hasn't disappeared. As she now writes her first book, she still asks herself: who will want to hear from me? Am I really the expert? But she keeps writing, 40,000 words and counting. And as she talks to others, she finds her voice affirmed again and again: maybe I do have something to say.

What makes Yasmeen a brilliant doubter is not that she banishes uncertainty but that she works with it. She demonstrates the essence of Active Doubt – using uncertainty as a catalyst, going back to her raw ingredients, seeking wisdom from others and moving forward one step at a time. In doing so, she finds her flow: facing her doubt, listening to what it tells her, opening up to new possibilities, and walking forward with purpose.

The joy of flow: how?

To find flow in doubt, we draw on both its energy and its purpose, using it as a way to work constructively: Face it, Listen to it, Open it up, and Walk forward – FLOW.

The doubtFLOW model: inspired by Csikzentmihalyi

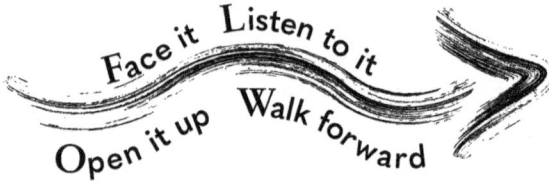

Figure 7: The doubtFLOW model

Flow step	Key focus	Guiding question
1. Face it.	Name the doubt. Understand the story. Discover why it matters.	*What am I doubting?* 'I doubt I am the right person to lead this big project.'
		Why is this important to me? 'I doubt I can lead this project, but it matters because I want to get ahead in my career.'
2. Listen to it.	Learn what doubt is asking of you. Respond with care.	*What is doubt asking of me?* 'What new skills do I need to develop to move forward?' 'What new challenge is it asking me to face and how might this help me in future?'
		How can I take care of me in this process? 'What mindset will support me right now? It is okay not to have all the answers currently.'

Flow step	Key focus	Guiding question
3. *Open it up.*	Get curious. Cross-examine it. Let others walk alongside you.	*What is the evidence?* 'What are the facts?' *Who can support me?* 'Who could coach or mentor me through this process?'
4. *Walk forward.*	Decide and do. Small steps lead forward to bigger future strides.	*What is my decision? What I am I going to do?* 'What concrete steps will I commit to in order to move this forward?'

Let's dive into each step of FLOW and explore how to apply it in practice:

Face it

Start by naming your doubt. Labelling the doubt brings it into conscious awareness – giving you a partner you can begin a dialogue with, instead of a shadow that silently controls you. Like looking at a picture on the wall: instead of it becoming all-consuming, we gain perspective.

It may need unpacking from the initial trigger to the internal triggers, by drilling down on each statement, using the *why ladder* – by repeatedly asking why to help us drill down. For example:

What am I doubting?

- The initial trigger: 'I am worried that my manager does not think I am competent enough to deliver the integration of the new software system.' (Tied to a relationship.)

Why is that?

- The internal trigger: 'Because I know I didn't do a good enough job on the last project, compared with my peers.' (Tied to a story.)

Why was that?

- The internal trigger: 'Because I don't think I am smart enough.' (Tied to a belief.)

Why does this matter to me?

- Purpose provides motivation: 'Expertise in this new software system will open more options for me from a career perspective. I want to create options, as ultimately I want to be able to work nearer my family.'

As James Park, founder of Fitbit, puts it:

> *'I think you need to have conviction about what you are doing... really have inner conviction, and if it means going against what others think, you should take that leap.'*[4]

When our doubts feel overwhelming, anchoring ourselves in a personal mission gives us the courage to take bold action.

Purpose lights the pathway for doubt. It gives it guardrails and a place to walk towards, with positive momentum. Our purpose is something bigger than ourselves. It forces us to take the high ground and use our self-doubts constructively.

My own experience is that finding your personal purpose can tie you into knots. We expect a eureka moment – *this* is what it is! Yes, sometimes that happens, when there a life jolt moment, one that wakes people up to their purpose. But for most of us it is something that takes time to find. In one of my early coach trainings with Robert Holden PhD, he said 'just pick one.' Commit to something – make a difference. What is the worst that can happen? If it's not right, life has a way of autocorrecting and nudging you in a different direction and that 'misstep' may well lay the foundations for what's to come.

If you know your personal purpose then you can see how the challenge in your doubt links to that.

Brilliant doubter: Natalia, Board Member

Natalia began her career at a major fashion retailer, as a 16-year-old on Oxford Street. Nearly three decades later, she had lived and worked around the world – eventually serving on the company's board.

She planned to study geography at university. Her passion for the subject was inspired by her grandfather; whilst taking care of his land, he had also seen himself as the custodian of it. School had different plans for her. They told her she was not performing and would not get an A grade – they doubted her ability. This doubt lit a fire in Natalia. She went on to get her A and achieved the highest grade in the class. 'I deliberately did less of what they wanted me to do and studied more at home to counteract this. All I needed them for was to sit the exam.'

This was 'away from' motivation aligned with Natalia's purpose: 'I like being the underdog and fighting for the underdog. I care deeply about justice and equity, because it is very easy to pigeonhole people. It inspires my fight mechanism.'

'There was doubt that I could achieve anything when I was asked to go to Hong Kong for the business, even though I had only just done my MBA. It was kind of like, "oh, you just go and play over there and whether you succeed or don't succeed, it isn't a big risk for the company".' Succeed she did.

Discovery questions

Natalia found what mattered to her; doubt activated her. *Why is this important to you?* Create a rich and meaningful response to this question. It may require a few sentences, to build a vision of why it is important. When you have achieved it, imagine you are playing a mini movie in your head – what would it show? Consider:

* What would you be thinking when you achieve this?

* What would you be doing when you achieve this?

* How would you feel when you achieve this?

* What would you see yourself doing in that moment?

* What would it pave the way for in the future?

Listen to it

Doubt can sound like truth. 'I can't do this.' 'They don't think I'm good enough.' 'I'll fail.' But these are stories – not facts. Instead, consider:

What is the challenge that doubt is asking of me?

In this way, doubt becomes less of an enemy to silence and more of a trusted advisor whose questions stretch us. I had a client who had been given some tough feedback on her influencing style, and rather than challenging it she made it her goal to make influencing her superpower. After two months the Regional VP asked her line manager what had he done to her, as she seemed like a different person. His reply: 'She listened to the feedback.' The reframe had almost immediate impact.

Try the *reframing formula*:

Instead of [assumption], I choose to see [new perspective].

For example, instead of thinking, 'I can't do this new integration programme, I choose to see it as a chance to build my networking and influencing skills'.

Or ask yourself:

- What is this doubt trying to protect me from?
- What if the opposite were true?
- What if this challenge helps me to become more of who I want to be?

Assumptions are light dimmers. They wrap around our beliefs and keep us in the dark. Curiosity is how we switch the light back on.

Respond with care

Whilst we are making the case for the brilliance in doubt, we need to acknowledge that it can be emotionally draining and challenging. An element of self-care is required.

Consider:

- How can I show compassion to myself in this situation?
- What is a more compassionate version of the thought I am having?
- If someone I cared about felt this way, what would I say to them?

Open it up

Doubt is a mischief maker; you must smile at it, as it plays with us.

The irony of doubt is that it encourages us to feel certain about our uncertainty. You couldn't make it up. Self-doubt has a habit of masquerading as truth, presenting as a fact – 'I doubt I can present as well as my colleagues.' 'I doubt my concerns about the project are valid.' 'I am not good enough to have a seat at this table.' Our brain interprets the sentence as a truth which must be believed. And yet, the very presence of doubt in the statement is an invitation to doubt the belief, and open it up.

Never ask a question you know the answer to came from my work with Claire Pedrick – the Coaches' Coach. Doubt is asking a question – and our job is to stay curious about what it's really saying.

Cross-examine your doubt

While doubt has many strengths, it isn't always helpful – especially when it remains too vague to be understood or acted on. It thrives on generalizations. A generalization is when we make a sweeping statement and apply the thinking across everything: 'I am not good enough.' 'I will never be promoted.' 'I will never get a job as good as the one I have just been let go from.' The partnership is in specificity – doubt invites us to bring evidence to the table, to co-examine whether the story it's telling us is true.

What are the facts? What is the pattern? What is the exception?

John was the master of change, someone who kept reinventing his career. Trained in the US as a lawyer, he worked in entertainment, switched into marketing, and developed a new skillset in data. Highly creative, with side hustles always on the go, he planned to relocate back to the US that summer – another change, another adventure. However, there was a change he hadn't foreseen: his role was being made redundant. John identified he was experiencing the grief curve and the emotional rollercoaster that it was – the anger, the fear, and the knock to his self-esteem. Why me? Did they not rate me? Am I not good enough? His self-doubt was alive. We got curious and looked at the evidence:

How is the company currently performing?

o   *Poorly.*

How did the new strategic direction of the company impact his role?

o   *Changing direction meant that there were now too many people in his area.*

What feedback had he received previously about his performance?

o *There were some development areas, but nothing to suggest he was being managed out.*

If the company didn't rate him, why would they invest in his coaching (it had been approved only six weeks before)?

o *They wouldn't.*

How would he describe the journey he took during the time he spent in role – from where he began to where he got to?

o *It started with understanding the data and transforming the strategy. I have built the equivalent of a house from it with solid foundations and processes in place.*

By the last question his self-doubt had loosened its grip.

Try asking:

* What data contradicts my fear?

* When have I handled something like this before?

* What did you do to make it happen?

You are not a one-hit wonder; if you can do it in one area of your life, or at one time, then there is the possibility that you can do it again.

Use 'what if?' to disrupt the spiral

Brutal breakups between individuals and organizations tend to be a speciality for executive coaches – and I'm no exception. People often feel like they've been spat out of the corporate machine unfairly: the casualty of a personality clash, a political land grab, or an impersonal restructure. Even when that's not strictly the case, it can still feel brutal – and scarring to the psyche.

I had one brilliant client whose exit was dragging painfully on. Despite everything, he was negotiating brilliantly – reaching into the organization, building bridges and new connections, finding ways to buy time through additional projects, and strengthening his profile as he went. It was textbook: a masterclass in how to leave well.

He eventually ended up on gardening leave just as he was finalizing the offer for a brilliant new job – one that played to his strengths, elevated his reputation, and delivered a little sweet revenge to his previous employer. A happy ending, but throughout, he was plagued with doubts. Understandably so.

We did several coaching sessions, and in one particularly despairing moment, I asked him, 'What if you get something even better?' I've rarely felt more joy in getting to say, 'I told you so' when it happened.

In truth, it was his doubt that helped him. It fuelled a systematic, measured approach to handling the situation – with the rigour of a scientist and the precision of an accountant. Collaborating, creating, working the problem. Doubt didn't stop him – it opened the possibility of something better.

Ask yourself:

- What if this is the first step towards something bigger?
- If you were advising a friend or colleague in this situation, what would you encourage them to think, feel, and do?
- If you have handled something like this before – what might you have learnt from it?

Curiosity keeps us in dialogue with our self-doubt. A conversation that seeks to understand, to explore, and get to new thinking.

Don't go it alone

We tend to dine out with self-doubt alone. Locking it in our heads, willing it not to escape, and tormenting ourselves by constantly staring at it. Isolating. A group of chief encouragers – collaborators, mentors, and coaches – guards against this. When doubt is witnessed by another, it can bring additional wisdom. They notice what is unsaid, ignored, and misinterpreted.

Try this:

- *Create a personal board of encouragers.* Create a board who are there to encourage you to move forward and challenge too. Assign informal roles, for example, Insight Expert, Connector, Personal Development Director and so on… there is no reason why you can't have a Chief Entertainment Officer.

- *Find a coach and/or mentor.* To bring challenge to your doubts, and support you. A coach will encourage you to flow through your doubts using questions to encourage self-reflection and action, while a mentor will share their insights with you and act as a wise sounding-board.

Questions to help find a coach who is a good fit for you:

- What clients/briefs do you work best with? And less well with?

- If I were being coached by you, what would I experience?

- Do you provide supervision for your coaching? (Supervision provides rigour, challenge, and focus on doing the best thing by clients.)

Mentors can provide fuel for our progression. Often, people get a mentor and have interesting conversations with them, but to maximize their potential, more deliberate intention and structure helps.

Questions to maximize a mentor relationship:

Focus area	Purpose	Example questions
Mentor insights	Gain wisdom from your mentor's experience and career.	• What do you wish you had known at my stage of life or career? • What are you learning right now? • What is the most important leadership lesson you have learned?

Focus area	Purpose	Example questions
Self-awareness	Generate insights about yourself and your development.	• What obstacle – that I don't see – is holding me back? • What must I do to overcome it and keep growing? • If I focused on one development area, which would have the biggest impact on my success?
Situational	Address a specific challenge you're facing right now.	• I've given feedback to a direct report and it hasn't landed – what should I try next? • I'm presenting to the executive team next week – what do I need to know about them to make my message land? • I've been told to be 'more strategic' – what specific shifts would demonstrate that?
Skill development	Build targeted capabilities identified from your reflections and feedback.	• What are your top three tips to develop this skill? • If you were in my role, how would you go about developing this over the next 90 days?

Face the compliments

Are you an Avid Compliment Avoider? There's an art to dodging compliments. We shift the conversation, shrink our presence, or physically move away to avoid letting praise land. I caught myself doing exactly that – walking up the stairs away from someone mid-compliment and pretending not to hear. A missed chance to strengthen self-belief.

Pete Markey, Chief Marketing Officer, won Marketer of the Year, at an award ceremony in 2023. As the formalities ended, the Editor of *Marketing Week* predicted what Pete would do next: 'You're going to spend the whole evening saying it's not about me, it's about the team. For once, Pete – just shut up and listen.' That moment landed. Facing the compliments allowed Pete to rewrite some old doubt-driven narratives.

Discovery questions

- Why do I ignore compliments?
- When do I accept them – and when don't I? What's the difference?
- What might I be avoiding by deflecting praise?
- What if I fully received the next compliment I'm given?
- Write it down. Then ask:
  o How does this change what I believe about myself?
  o Where else might this already be true?

Let the compliments land.

Walk forward

What steps am I going to take now?
Whilst we can decide to move forward, how to do so can be a challenge. It can feel like a whole continent that you have to trek across with no money, no phone, no transport, and only one pair of trainers. An ill-prepared expedition, where you are not sure exactly where you want to end up, and what resources you have to get there.

How to get started walking forward? By chunking the challenge down into actionable steps. Chunking allows you to zoom in and out of the doubt. When you chunk up it elevates your thinking to a higher level. Chunking down is when you break it into smaller pieces. Both routes can help to break it into manageable steps:

Chunking up questions:

* What are the high-level phases that you need to complete walking forward? (e.g., identify the team, co-create the vision, create the plan, create buy-in to the process.)
* If I zoomed out and looked at this from a year ahead, what would be important?
* What is the ultimate goal or purpose behind this?
* What would this look like if it were simple?

Chunking down questions:

* What is the first step I need to take?
* What does success look like when I take that step?
* What is a component of this?
* Who/what/where specifically?

We can walk forward, even if we do not know the whole path, as long as we take the first step.

What is my decision?

Jeff Bezos talks about making 'two door' and 'one door' decisions. A one door decision has significant impact because there is no other door to walk back through if it's the wrong decision. Launching Amazon Prime would be an example – once introduced it would be hard to backtrack from this. With two door decisions there are alternative pivots if it does not work out. Bezos invested all his time in one door decisions and delegated the two door decisions.

Decide. Move. Adjust if needed. As long as you are walking, you are progressing.

Self-doubt doesn't disappear when we move – it is reshaped. When we walk forward, even a little, we invite new evidence in, new data about who we are becoming. FLOW doesn't eliminate doubt and we would not want it to. FLOW helps us to partner with doubt. And when doubt has a direction, it no longer holds us back. It helps us move.

Doubt distilled: with FLOW

* *FLOW turns doubt into direction.* Framing, Listening, Opening, Walking – this model gives doubt a route forward. Instead of circling endlessly, we find clarity and progression. Doubt becomes not a block, but a bridge.

* *Face it: Doubt is not a flaw – it's a signal.* When we *face* our doubts, we recognize that they show up when something matters. Doubt isn't failure – it's the mind's way of asking, 'Are you paying attention?' Naming it starts the transformation.

* *Listen to it: Doubt carries a challenge.* When we *listen* with curiosity, doubt reveals what it's asking of us – to stretch, risk, or learn. What new skill is it inviting you to develop? What growth lies on the other side of this discomfort?

* *Open it up: Doubt transforms in the light of exploration.* When we *open up* the doubt, we loosen its grip. Question it. Cross-examine it. Invite support and creativity into the mix. Doubt loves generalizations – specificity dissolves them.

* *Walk forward: Action reshapes the story.* Doubt doesn't need to disappear for you to move. When we *walk forward* with even a small step, we shift the narrative. Confidence is built by movement, not certainty.

> *Care is the current that carries you through FLOW.*
>
> Each stage of FLOW asks something of us – and compassion is what sustains us. Doubt can be heavy; self-kindness keeps us afloat. What would it look like to support yourself as you would a friend?

But, what to do if the doubt resides outside of you?

'In all affairs it's a healthy thing now and then to hang a question mark on the things you have long taken for granted.'

- Bertrand Russell

part three

Situational Doubt

Chapter 8:
Situational doubt: when the questions come from the outside

'What do we need to do to accelerate growth again?'

'The board is asking us to cut costs by 30%, where can we make these cuts?'

'The innovation pipeline is weak; how can we turbocharge this to outpace our competitors?'

These high-stake questions came from the outside and were pressing down on the leader I was working with – strategic, urgent, and laced with expectation. But underneath these was a quieter, more personal question: 'Have I got the right team to deliver what we need to achieve?'

This is situational doubt in action – not born from personal insecurity but sparked by specific external factors. The kind of doubt that might arise from changing contexts, shifting goals, or the behaviour of others. In this case, the leader wasn't doubting himself – at least, not at first. He was doubting if, given the colossal complexity of the challenge, his team could be expected to rise to it.

Some of the team members were the emotional heartbeat of the company – loyal, hardworking, and committed to deliver what they thought the business needed. But the business had moved on.

Growth had slowed. Board pressure was mounting. The leader's unspoken doubts began to seep into team dynamics. Tension surfaced. Trust frayed. At the heart of it was a single, sharp question: *can this individual do what is needed in the next phase of the business?*

The kind of question that lives between people. Doubt can be contagious. When a leader silently questions someone's capability, the other person will often sense it. This unspoken tension can lead them to doubt themselves – or, just as often, to distrust the leader in return. Silence can breed mistrust.

Situational doubt had given way to self-doubt. The leader began to ask: 'Is it possible I'm contributing to the tension I'm trying to resolve?' That question forced a pause. A reckoning. A chance to examine how they might need to show up differently to shift the behaviours of the team. The edges of doubt blur, as we oscillate between the situational and the self. It starts on the outside and can quietly move inward. The doubt doesn't always originate within, but it can end up there, blurring the lines between the two forms of doubt.

The difference between self- and situational doubt lies in where the core struggle sits:

- *Self-doubt*

  The root is internal and often tied to identity.

  > 'I have to present to the board, and I'm afraid I'll be exposed as not capable enough.'

  >> ⇒ Underneath: 'Because I'm not smart.'

- *Situational doubt*

  The root is external and tied to the dynamics of the moment.

  > 'I have to present to the board, and I'm worried the COO will resist because the strategy threatens his budget and power.'

  >> ⇒ Underneath: the doubt is driven by the context, not by self-worth.

Discovery questions

- What are you currently doubting at work and what's happening around you that might be shaping this doubt?

- What external factors – context, data, relationships, or decisions – might be influencing how this situation feels?

- What external factors might be driving others' doubts about this situation?

- How might what you're learning from this doubt change your next steps?

- Could this doubt be a signal for dialogue, rather than an obstacle to overcome?

Whilst situational doubt is not personal in nature, leaders often keep it to themselves, feeling a duty towards the people they are leading to project certainty and to keep them focused on where they are going, and also, sometimes, to minimize concerns. They have a professional responsibility: the desire to protect their people, safeguard outcomes, and live up to the weight of their role. Leaders may think, 'I have got 10,000 people working for me; if we don't get this right, a whole bunch of people are going to lose their jobs, if not all of them.' The stakes can be high.

Professional Doubt is part of professional responsibility. A responsibility to deliver for the business and its people. And that responsibility includes the courage to pause, to question, and to use that insight to find a better way forward. Doubt, when held well, is not indecision – it's due diligence. A sign that you care about the consequences, not just the outcomes.

The four kinds of situational doubt

Most often, situational doubt surfaces in four areas: when the environment changes (context), when the information is unclear (data), when trust wavers (relationships), or when the right path is uncertain (decisions). These make up the situational doubt framework: CDRD.

Diving into each one:

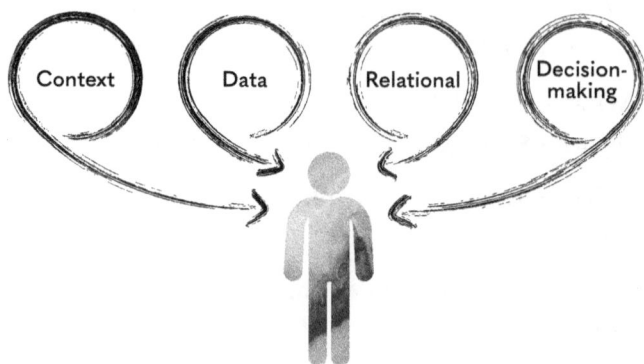

Figure 8: Situational doubt framework (C.D.R.D.)

Contextual doubt: when the rules shift without warning

Imagine waking up and realizing the rules of the game have changed, such as the unexpected and unpredictable nature of the USA's tariff policy on goods and services. That's contextual doubt. It doesn't come from within, but from the shifting ground beneath us – a new boss, a restructured team, a volatile market, a change in how decisions get made.

In coaching, I often say context is king. The same question asked in a founder-led startup will land differently than in a global matrixed business. The context shapes what matters, what's expected, and what kind of leadership will thrive. And when that context shifts – even slightly – the doubts often arrive.

We may have felt confident last month. But now the growth target has doubled. A key stakeholder has exited. Or we've moved into a role where the culture runs on unspoken rules we don't yet understand. Doubt surfaces, not because we've changed, but because the backdrop has.

You might recognize this kind of doubt in moments like these:

- 'I doubt the team can deliver what's needed next quarter – we've just lost three people and we're running on 87% capacity.'

* 'In my last role, I knew how to get sign-off. Here, the founders make the decisions, and I doubt I can influence them as they have such strong opinions.'

Sometimes, contextual doubt blends with other forms of Professional Doubt. A changing landscape can expose missing data, strain relationships, or push us towards difficult decisions. Like in this scenario:

> *'Our biggest competitor is launching a new product just before ours. It's aimed at the same market, but we don't know its full feature set [data doubt]. I'm not sure the sales lead will raise concerns – they tend to spin things [relational doubt]. And now I need to decide whether we move our launch forward, even though testing isn't complete [decision-making doubt].'*

Contextual doubt rarely travels alone. When the environment shifts, it often brings data gaps, tensions in relationships, and tough decisions in its wake – showing just how interconnected doubt can be.

Discovery questions

* How has the context shifted since you began this role or project?

* Which contextual changes might be shaping your stakeholders' responses?

* What shifts are the team consciously or unconsciously ignoring?

* Where do you still have influence, even as the context evolves?

Data doubt: what are the numbers really saying?

Sometimes doubt doesn't come from people or pressure – it comes from the numbers. Or rather, from what's missing, inconsistent, or unclear within them.

Data doubt shows up when the facts don't quite hold
A figure seems off. A report doesn't reflect reality on the ground. A forecast is missing a critical variable. You don't know if the information is flawed, or if you're just seeing it from the wrong angle – but something feels shaky.

More recently, even the major institutions we rely on for data have expressed doubts about the reliability of their own figures. In 2023, the UK Office for National Statistics delayed releasing the labour market data for this very reason.[1] When facts falter, a vacuum forms; one that makes it hard to plan policy, which in turn ripples through to organisations' own decision-making and planning.

This kind of doubt can slow momentum. Decisions stall, questions multiply, and trust – both in the data and in the people behind it – can start to fray. When the information is incomplete, the picture is incomplete. And in high-stakes environments, that kind of uncertainty can be hard to carry.

You might notice it in moments like these:

- 'You've estimated the unit cost at £3.97, but what happens if we shift production to South Africa?'

- 'Your proposal doesn't account for our competitor's usual Q4 product launch – without that, I'm not confident in the marketing assumptions.'

- 'Last year we put in more people, more money, more tech than your numbers show – what's missing?'

When the data is questioned, the person presenting it is often questioned too. That's the quiet undercurrent of data doubt – it's rarely just about the spreadsheet. It's about the credibility behind it. And when that credibility wobbles, relationships can feel less secure too.

Data doubt doesn't just ask 'What's true?'

It often asks, 'Can I trust what I've been given – and the person who gave it to me?'

Brilliant doubter: Edmund, Director of Legal

Edmund was new in the organization. When I had worked with him previously, I was always struck by his intelligence, razor sharp focus to deliver, and an energy that runs towards life with arms open – whether it was with his busy family, community work, or continuous learning (he recently had done more legal exams) – and now he had landed a challenging new legal role. A brilliant doubter. It was Christmas, there was an issue with the company accounts, something had been missed. The key question was whose responsibility was it – the Finance Director's or his? Of course, the FD thought it was Edmund's.

Over Christmas, it took residency in his mind, as he wondered what else he had missed. Paradoxically, he also tried to avoid the issue by asking his team to investigate it. A self-confessed avoidance strategy. A strategy to avoid his deep-down concern that he was not up to his new job. The imposter had arrived as an unwanted Christmas guest. However, the root of his doubt stemmed from the missing data – what legally should have been included in the accounts, what was in the accounts, what was missing, and, most importantly, whose responsibility was it?

He found a solution for the accounts and recognized his avoidance strategy of outsourcing the worry to his team. He also had new 'data' on the FD and a plan of how to manage him going forward with eyes wide open.

Even when it's about numbers, data doubt doesn't always add up cleanly. The figures may be binary – but the meaning behind them rarely is. The pressure from the numbers triggered an internal 'coping' strategy – avoidance.

Discovery questions

- Where is the data incomplete, inconsistent, or missing altogether?

- What assumptions might be shaping how the data is being presented or interpreted?

- To what extent is your doubt about the data itself, versus the person delivering it?

- What additional information would give you the confidence to move forward?

Relational doubt: what is the issue between us?

I had a client who was frequently at odds with her line manager, even though her relationships across the wider business were strong. Her department had recently been praised in an audit. Her work was clearly valued – but the tension with her manager remained.

He micro-managed her, treated her differently to her peers, and their working relationship was thick with mutual distrust. It wasn't a one-sided dynamic – both of them were caught in a loop of defensiveness and distance.

In one coaching session, she said plainly, 'I think he's going to try and exit me.' I wasn't sure. They had clashed before, and I wondered if this was part of their familiar pattern. But she insisted the signals felt different this time. Meetings were happening without her. Information wasn't being shared.

She was right. Not long after, her role was made redundant.

The twist? She was ready. She had already gathered evidence, consulted legal advice, and walked into the process well prepared, resulting in an exceedingly healthy exit package. Her relational doubt – as uncomfortable as it was – had tuned her into what was unfolding before it was ever spoken aloud.

Relational doubt lives in the space between people. Left unacknowledged, it can erode trust, weaken collaboration, and stall progress. But when noticed and explored, it can also act as an early warning system – a signal that something is shifting, even if no one's said it out loud yet.

Relational doubt often arises from a mix of styles, past experiences, power imbalances, or unspoken expectations. It's subjective. Messy. And it can feel intensely personal. Especially when one person holds more positional power – doubt can grow in the silences, in the micro-signals, in what's withheld.

When doubt takes root in a relationship, it doesn't just stay between two people. It ripples outward – into how people collaborate, what they share, what they withhold, and how safe it feels to speak the truth.

You might notice it in moments like these:

- 'Amit has recently been promoted to the next level, he is ambitious, and I don't trust him to do the right thing by his team.'

- 'I can't trust Katie to do the work to a high-enough standard based on what she delivered when I worked with her previously.'

- 'I am concerned that my team is not strong enough to deliver the change that the business is looking for.'

Discovery questions

- Who are you finding yourself doubting right now?

- What past experiences or stories might be colouring how you see them?

- How is that doubt shaping the way you show up with them and the way they show up with you?

- What might shift if you changed your approach?

Decision-making doubt: not sure what to do

A client was struggling to decide whether to stay with an early-stage start-up or move on and find a new role. She believed in the market potential of the business proposition but not in the current product proposition. They were in the position of getting next round funding and were using her name and experience as part of the offer to get the funding, adding to the pressure for her to decide sooner rather than later. Alongside this, she had concerns that the founder was controlling, and she was unsure how much she could influence him. She saw two paths: fight to influence the founder and unlock potential – or cut her losses and move on. A tough call, as nothing was certain at this early stage.

This was a classic dilemma – an 'either or' decision. A common challenge. The two choices are often mutually exclusive, where choosing one prevents the other. Often, it's the doubts that lead to the dilemma, and the opinions gather around the two viewpoints. As we weigh up the options, it is our doubt that can intensify, making it harder to reconcile the dilemma and get to a decision. How to unlock dilemmas will be addressed in Chapter 10.

The challenge to make a decision might be because the other forms of doubt are at play too. We may be struggling to make a decision because we are finding it hard to forecast the next three years' sales due to the volatile trading environment (contextual); we have a poor relationship with the marketing and innovation teams, which is diminishing our trust in the project (relational); and the data points forming the assumptions for the modelling are weak. All of this is making it hard to make a recommendation and decision for what the business should invest in.

Discovery questions

- What decision are you wrestling with right now?

- What makes this decision difficult: lack of clarity, too many options, fear of the consequences?

- What would you advise someone else to do if they were in your situation?

- What one step could you take to move this decision forward?

In many ways, decision-making doubt is the culmination of Professional Doubt: it's where the external complexities (context, data, and relationships) converge and require a choice. The very act of deciding under pressure is a professional skill – and one that doubt often sharpens, if we let it.

Can you have too much situational doubt?

Yes and no – ironically.

Situational doubt exists on a spectrum, with tension holding the two ends. At one end, it fuels curiosity and insight, and when that is coupled with a desire to move forward it creates a healthy tension, adding value in a professional context. But left unresolved, it can curdle into something more corrosive.

When situational doubt is ignored or unresolved over time, it can harden into cynicism. Cynicism is the equivalent of tying people's hands behind their backs. Its purpose is to disable and disarm, not to seek resolution. It is stalled Active Doubt. Do people start off as cynical? Or does cynicism grow because their experiences and thinking, which created the doubts, have not been listened to?

When I worked for Nokia, we restructured globally every year. It created chaos. We would spend six months working out how to make the new structure work and get things done, and then the rumble of change would come, gradually getting louder, leading to distraction and a lack of productivity. By the time we got to my last restructure I was cynical. My cynicism was not constructive and ultimately brought closure to my time at Nokia. I experienced what Wanous, Reichers, and Austin (2000) explored in their study 'Cynicism About Organizational Change'.[2] It covered the pessimistic viewpoints people can have about the success of organizational change efforts, alongside the distrust of leaders who are driving the change. In my case: do we really need to do this all over again so soon after the last time? Doubt can become entrenched. Doubt for doubt's sake. It needs a purpose.

It can often feel like there is one team member who has 'too much doubt' – the voice of constant challenge, the derailer of meetings. And with team consensus the voice can be ignored. However, if you ignore it, are you losing the wisdom and challenge that doubt brings?

We'll explore how to work with situational doubt – rather than push it aside – in Chapter 10, including practical tools like 'doubt meetings' and thinking models that help surface unseen perspectives.

Doubt distilled: when the questions come from the outside

- *Situational doubt begins on the outside.* It's sparked by changes in context, relationships, information, or demands – not by personal insecurity. It's a reaction to the professional world shifting around us.

- *It often leads inward.* Though situational doubt starts externally, it can quietly stir self-doubt. The edges blur: 'Is this about the context, or about me?'

- *There are four core forms: contextual, data, relational, and decision-making.* These often overlap – what starts as a context shift may uncover flawed data, strain relationships, or force tough choices. Doubt rarely travels alone.

- *Unexplored doubt can curdle into cynicism.* When situational doubt is left unspoken or unresolved, it can harden. Doubt without a path forward doesn't just stall progress – it can disengage and divide.

> * *Engaged with well, situational doubt sharpens our leadership.* When we treat it as a signal – rather than a threat – doubt can prompt deeper insight, wiser judgment, and more intentional action. It's not an obstacle to avoid but a tension to work with.

If situational doubt is a signal, what is at risk if we ignore it – and what could shift if we learned to use it?

Chapter 9:
Finding the brilliance: the power in situational doubt

Missing the power of situational doubt is like working in a dimly lit room: we can move, but we risk tripping over what's right in front of us. Embracing situational doubt flips the light switch – it clears the fog of bias and reveals the subtle shifts happening around us. Situational doubt needs light, so the shiny façade on the surface drops away, and we see what's *really* going on – making new, sharper connections as a result.

The Beyond Meat business needed more doubt. Founder Ethan Brown's vision for the business was pioneering at the time: building 'meat' from plants. A potentially brilliant proposition. Brown partnered early on with Dr Fu-hung Hsieh and Dr Harold Huff, food scientists who had developed a plant-based meat prototype. Their technology shaped Beyond Meat's first products. They attracted high profile investors, including Bill Gates and Leonardo DiCaprio, and at one point the stock price surged 800% above the initial offering. However, all did not stay well for long. There were key missteps:

- To accelerate growth, they partnered with KFC and McDonalds, assuming their products would quickly become meat substitutions, but this did not happen. The early adopters' buy-in failed to translate into wider appeal for the product.

- The product was significantly more expensive than beef, and the majority of consumers were unwilling to pay this premium.

In 2022, revenue had stalled and the stock value dropped significantly. Early success had created overconfidence and their focus on scientific expertise had resulted in the misread of consumer wants. If they had created more space for situational doubt, they may have course-corrected by asking questions sooner:

- Was the world truly ready to mass adopt this new premium food technology (contextual doubt)?

- Was the modelling in the pilot metrics robust enough to take in different scenarios (data doubt)?

- Are we truly listening to what retail partners and customers are saying about the taste and price (relational doubt)?

- Are we scaling too fast? How could we test different hypotheses before launching nationwide campaigns (decision-making doubt)?

This science-based business would have benefited from the wise wisdom of Sir Antony Gormley, the British artist and sculptor – 'Doubt is one of the engines of truth.'[1] Truth would have allowed them to see *beyond (their own) meat.*

Whereas self-doubt matures the individual, situational doubt matures the organization. An organization matures by looking beyond itself, scanning both the internal and external landscape in search of what is true in this moment. That maturity comes from letting go of a fixed ego: the belief that our current view is the only view, our current plan the only path. Instead, situational doubt invites a willingness to admit we might have this wrong, a willingness to recognize that it is the collective wisdom of the organization that will shape what is needed now and next. Jeremy Borys, Chief Talent Officer of Alix Partners, puts it powerfully:

'If you seek expertise, power, or control, then doubt has a different meaning to you, but if you are seeking wisdom, I think doubt has a huge role to play because the more you can doubt, the more you can understand the patterns of your doubt and challenge your assumptions, and the wiser you become.'[2]

And the wiser the organization becomes as well.

This collective wisdom shows up in three key ways:

1. Contextual agility.
2. Organizational alignment.
3. Decision quality.

These are the three ways situational doubt becomes a source of collective strength – and we'll explore each in turn.

Contextual agility

Contextual agility is the ability to read the room and respond to what has changed. It's the need to re-contextualize, to question whether old assumptions still hold, and to pivot when needed. In 2023 Unity, a gaming engine software company, failed to do this when it announced a new 'Runtime Fee' policy. It charged gaming developers a fee for each game installation after certain thresholds were met. There was an immediate backlash from the gaming community. The gamers' trust in Unity was broken. It led to long-term reputational damage, despite Unity retracting the policy and the CEO stepping down. Sam Barlow, a creator of games, said at the time there was 'a sense of Unity being on the wrong path for a while, and this moment really took it to a new level.'[3]

The following questions would have been helpful to ask before launching the policy:

- What has changed around us?
- Do the rules we have operated by still apply?
- What assumptions no longer make sense?
- What do customers currently need and expect from us?

They would have seen the shifts that had happened in the gaming developer ecosystem – creators had more options now, and they expected the company to continue democratizing game development by making it more accessible, as their original mission had stated. The change in policy did not do this. The developers, who were internal advocates, had pushed back on the policy before it was live. They had given voice to the doubt in this situation, which leads to more questions:

- Which stakeholders' voices do we need to consider?

- And who, if anyone, have we ignored?

As we saw earlier in the book, to make sense of a complex, changing world, the BANI framework – Brittle, Anxious, Nonlinear, and Incomprehensible – is helpful. Situational doubt provides a constructive force to apply to these four conditions:

BANI	What is it?	The role of situational doubt
Brittle	Systems can appear strong but are rigid and prone to sudden collapse when stressed. When the massive container ship *Ever Given* became stuck in the Suez Canal, it held up about 12% of global trade, causing huge delays in global supply chains, all coming from one ship's error. One small disruption can fracture an entire system.	The doubt muscle can help leaders to probe for fragilities in systems, and build resilience into the system, such as by creating contingency plans, or by diversifying. Here, situational doubt can be preventative. By asking: • Are we acting on outdated assumptions? • Where are we over-reliant and exposed?

BANI	What is it?	The role of situational doubt
Anxious	Constant changes and threats can lead to stress, unease, and reactive behaviour in both people and the system. This is often the outcome when a major change programme is announced, resulting in both stress and paralysis for a period of time.	Doubt plays a dual role here – it can fuel the anxiety if left unspoken, or soothe it when voiced and normalized, providing an opportunity to express what the person is truly thinking and feeling. This helps ease their feelings and create a greater sense of calm. By asking: • Help me to understand what you are experiencing right now. • What does the organization need to do to support you?
Nonlinear	The relationship between cause and effect is no longer predictable nor proportional, making it harder to model and anticipate. A single decision – like the introduction of US trade tariffs – can send shockwaves through entirely unrelated industries, such as a small West Coast hotel suddenly seeing a slump in peak-season bookings.	Doubt fuels test-and-learn strategies, driving agility into the system. It is adaptive and entrepreneurial – by flexing around what were once fixed plans or assumptions. By asking: • How can we pivot? • Are we still solving the right problem? • What is no longer serving us? • Where has the ground shifted without us noticing?

BANI	What is it?	The role of situational doubt
Incomprehensible	Complexity can make it difficult or impossible, at times, to fully understand what is happening, leading to confusion and poor decision-making. This was experienced in the UK business community post-Brexit, as politicians tried to negotiate deals, and businesses tried to figure out how to operate in this new world.	No one person can deal with all the complexity. Situational doubt invites multiple perspectives to the table, encouraging humility and collaboration. It avoids oversimplification. By asking: • Who else do we need to bring to our table? • What external thinking from other markets or industries would be helpful here?

Situational doubt gives us the edge in a brittle, anxious, nonlinear, and incomprehensible world. But context alone doesn't drive change – people do. And that is where organizational alignment begins.

Organizational alignment

The only certainty in organizations is change, and to make the change work, organizational alignment is vital. It is the ability to stay attuned to changing needs across relationships, teams, and priorities in response to the external environment.

Without situational doubt, silent fractures and invisible silos begin to form inside organizations. This brings a hardening of positions, with power and politics at play. In the absence of this most human characteristic – the ability to surface our doubts – we humans retreat more into ourselves and further away from the collective endeavour. Doubt is the relational glue, because it encourages deep listening, invites honesty, and demands connection from the differing parts of the system. It is how alignment is not just talked about, but built.

My own 'doubt bell' rang when I was easily able to book time with both the CEO and COO of a large organization to gather 360-degree feedback on my client. These were extremely busy people – why was it so easy to get in their diaries?

Within minutes, the answer was clear: frustration. Deep frustration with my client, who was leading a unit. The business was underperforming, and the executive team expected boldness, pace, and leveraging synergies from the wider business. Instead, they saw a leader still operating in his own fiefdom – doing what had worked in the past, but out of sync with what was needed now.

The context had shifted. But he hadn't.

Situational doubt – across all four lenses – was absent:

- *Contextual*: he hadn't adjusted to the new strategic environment.

- *Relational*: trust with senior leaders was deteriorating.

- *Data*: the metrics didn't support his direction.

- *Decision-making*: he was unwilling to adapt his approach.

At first glance, this may seem like the story of a misaligned leader. But it was more nuanced than that. He had deep loyalty from his team, held significant market knowledge, and played a constructive role at the senior table. The problem wasn't his capability – it was the absence of shared alignment. And I say 'shared' deliberately.

If there had been more space for relational doubt – on both sides – the outcome might have been different. If I had supported him to *doubt himself* just enough to hear the organization's signals, or if the organization had engaged with his resistance more openly, the conversation might have shifted from frustration to realignment.

Instead, the bond was broken and he left – taking his insight, relationships, and potential with him.

But here's the truth: situational doubt is only useful when there is psychological safety. Without it, doubt stays silent. People hold back, protect themselves, and opt out of the conversations that matter most. Leaders who want to work with situational doubt must create the conditions for it – by sharing their own uncertainties, creating a non-judgmental space for others to do the same, and actively working through doubt together to get to a better place.

And that better place can be measured by the quality of the decisions being made.

Decision quality

'If people are not surfacing their doubts, they are just saying "yes great plan," you are likely to end up with something that is not as great as it could be.'

—Pam Burton, ex-COO of Funding Circle
and early employee of LOVEFiLM

In this process we test, adapt, and learn. This thoughtful action results in better decisions. Quality inputs lead to quality decisions. Active Doubt asks, how can we make this better? What have we missed? What do we need to pay attention to take this forward?

When people bring doubt into decision-making – openly and constructively – the quality of thinking deepens. Situational doubt acts as a guard against mediocrity: it unsettles, challenges, and sharpens collective judgment.

Situational doubt is a guard against mediocrity; it unsettles and challenges us to think deeper and differently.

Brilliant doubter: Stephen Maher, Chair of The Gate/MSQ

'When you're in a creative pitch process with a client, there's a moment when everything seems to crystallize. But sometimes, the night before, you know something's not right. It's not a big thing, but instinctively – it's off. It's hard to speak up at that point. People have worked for weeks. You risk creating last-minute panic. But you also know: if we don't change it, we won't win. So, you say: "I know we've put a lot into this – but this part is not working. We unfortunately need to change it."

'It's not about control. It's not about proving your power. It's about getting it right – because something inside you knows we haven't got there yet.'

Stephen's story is a powerful example of decision-making doubt – not as weakness, but as courage. The willingness to *interrupt consensus* in the service of the work.

Brilliant doubters trust their gut when something's not quite right. But more importantly, they speak up – even when it's uncomfortable. They don't do it for ego or control. They do it for truth. For quality. For impact.

Discovery questions

* What is your gut instinct trying to tell you about a specific situation?

* When have you listened to it and it has been right? How could you do this more often?

And that's what makes situational doubt not just a habit of better thinking – but a force for better outcomes.

Sarah Watt reminds us, decision quality is dynamic. In fast-moving contexts, leaders must continuously re-evaluate to get to quality decisions.

Brilliant doubter: Sarah Watt, CEO

Sarah leads a business that is the very definition of fast-scaling – for the past decade it has doubled in size almost every year. The pace of growth means it can feel like she is leading a new organization every six months. What worked yesterday no longer works today – and once again, they must pivot.

Two repeating questions guide her leadership:

- What phase is the business in now?

- What leadership behaviours does this moment require from me?

Each reflection prompts her to examine what is shifting – in the context, in the data, in her team, and in what new decisions the moment requires. To match this, she asks what leadership behaviours this requires from herself.

Discovery questions

Sarah is demonstrating the positive process of Active Doubt. This cycle of questioning shows why doubt must remain active. What are your answers to these questions?

Sarah's story reminds us that situational doubt becomes *Active Doubt* when it is consistently applied – not just to strategy, but to self, team, and context. It's what keeps leadership alive, evolving, and in service of what's needed *now*.

By using doubt as 'the engine of truth' to challenge existing narratives and assumptions, the organization matures. That maturity is built on a collective truth: success depends on staying attuned to context, daring to voice uncertainty, and using doubt to drive better decisions.

Situational doubt distilled: why we need it

- *Situational doubt switches on the light.* In uncertainty, we often keep moving – even when we can't see clearly. Situational doubt flips the switch. It sharpens perception, revealing shifts in context, behaviour, and expectations that we might otherwise miss.

- *It builds agility in the face of complexity.* In a brittle, anxious, nonlinear, and incomprehensible world, situational doubt helps leaders to adapt. It pushes us to update assumptions, test alternatives, and flex plans to meet the moment.

- *It aligns people, not just plans.* Without doubt, organizations harden. Silos form, trust erodes, and politics grow. Situational doubt keeps leaders relationally attuned – helping teams realign around what matters now.

- *It strengthens decision quality.* Doubt challenges lazy thinking and group consensus. It forces better questions, better input, and better judgment. It sharpens decisions – not through hesitation, but through precision.

- *It matures the organization.* Where self-doubt humbles the individual, situational doubt matures the system. It invites truth over certainty, learning over defensiveness, and collective wisdom over individual control.

- *It must be active – and safe.* Situational doubt only works when it's voiced. That requires psychological safety. Leaders must go first – naming their doubts and making space for others to do the same. That's how doubt becomes a tool for real-time change.

How can we turn situational doubt into action that moves us to a better place?

Chapter 10:
The 'do' in situational doubt I: how to steer through situational doubt

'When it seems like an obvious decision – when everyone is screaming yes – that is exactly the time to press pause and inject some doubt. As the leader, I am genuinely not interested in rushing to a conclusion.'
—Des Power, ex-Google Vice President,
MD Fitbit International

These are the times when a leader must steer – not away from doubt, but through it. Head on. Steering where doubt is surfaced, heard, and used to generate deeper insight.

To steer well, we need to focus on four aspects:

1. *Space.* How to create a supportive space for doubt to be surfaced

2. *Listen.* How to tune into our own and others' doubts

3. *Conversation.* How to engage in dialogue together to work through doubt

4. *Decision.* How to move beyond doubt to get to a clear decision

This chapter is focused on how to *start* steering – not towards a decision, but towards a space where doubt can surface and be explored. We will look at how to create supportive conditions, how to listen for doubt (even when it hides), and how to engage in dialogue that makes doubt useful. In Chapter 11, we turn our attention to practical tools which we can use to channel the conversation into a decision.

Creating a supportive space for situational doubt to be surfaced

A supportive space is where doubt is not only tolerated but welcomed, encouraged, and rewarded. Where the leader and the team understand they need to walk and sometimes wade through the doubt together. The doubt is active and a richer place is not available without it.

The foundation of a supportive space is psychological safety. The term was originally identified by Amy Edmondson,[1] Professor of Harvard Business School, in 'Psychological Safety and Learning Behaviour in Work Teams' (1999). She defines psychological safety as 'a belief that one will not be punished or humiliated for speaking up with ideas, questions, concerns, or mistakes' and as 'a climate where people are comfortable being and expressing themselves.'

To help us understand what makes this space work, Timothy R. Clark's *Four Stages of Psychological Safety*[2] offers a useful lens. Each stage deepens the team's ability to not just express doubt – but to *do something with it*.

- *Inclusion safety.* If people don't feel accepted, they'll protect themselves – doubt will stay buried. Support begins with belonging.

  o *Who tends to sit apart, stay quiet, or seem distracted – even if it doesn't look like exclusion?*

- *Learner safety.* When people feel safe to ask questions, explore, and fail, they begin to test their doubts and see them as sources of insight.

  o *When was the last time your team talked about failure? What was said – and how did you respond?*

- *Contributor safety.* A supportive space allows people to share their thinking, ideas, and observations – including those that sound uncertain or unfinished.

  o *What do you notice about how people contribute – are ideas offered as half-thoughts, with an open invitation for others to build?*

- *Challenger safety.* This is where doubt flourishes into brilliance. When people feel safe to challenge the status quo, surface dissent, or offer a tough insight, they become active stewards of the group's clarity and progress.

  o *How does the team respond to differences of opinion? Do challenges spark curiosity – or discomfort?*

A supportive space, then, isn't created in a single moment – it's cultivated as trust deepens. The goal isn't harmony, it's honesty. When a team reaches challenger safety, doubt becomes a lever for excellence.

It begins with the leader – and their own relationship to doubt. In my experience, leaders think they have created a safe space, but it is not always the case – this is noticeable when there is little disagreement in team meetings, or only a few active voices participating. Healthy teams challenge each other, exploring disagreements, encouraging all perspectives to be aired, and in doing so strengthen their collective thinking.

Discovery questions

- What happened when I last expressed my doubts to the team? What did I do? And what did the team do?

- What behaviours do I exhibit that promote doubt in the team?

- What behaviours might I display that prevent doubt from being surfaced?

- What questions can I ask to invite and support doubt in others?

- Which of my own doubts would be helpful to share about this situation?

A supportive space requires the leader to separate the doubts being raised from the person who is raising them. Otherwise, the person can be labelled the 'negative one', but there is often a kernel of truth in what they are saying. It requires the leader to hold the doubt objectively, by seeing the doubt as an entity in itself, rather than being attached to the person.

- Which part of the wider organizational system is this person's doubt representing?

This question looks at where the root of the doubt is coming from. Are they voicing the elephant in the room?

How the leader can build on this:

- If you, as the leader, were to build the argument for the point the person is making, what would it be?

- And what, from this argument, would be helpful to consider as you plan the next steps?

This activity can be practised with people in the public eye. Next time you hear someone speak whose views are different to your own, listen, and ask: what is the doubt that this person is asking me to see? Even when I am in full opposition mode, there is usually a grain of insight that can be garnered from their point of view. There is no risk of you changing political party, sports team, or core beliefs with this behaviour, but it will loosen the stranglehold of certainty we have on our own thoughts.

Listen: what does situational doubt sound like?

Even the most driven leaders must learn when to take off the blinkers.

Successful founders often have their cause burning through them, like thoroughbred horses trained to scale impossibly high jumps. Their blinkers – mission, urgency, belief – keep their eyes fixed on the next obstacle. But great leadership isn't just about momentum. It's about awareness.

That awareness often shows up as situational doubt. Not the kind that halts progress, but the kind that invites reflection: 'Am I still set up for the next stage?' 'Do I have the right structure and skills in the business?' 'What's shifting around me that I'm not seeing?'

Or put another way: 'What's the feedback I'm resisting because it challenges what I want to believe?' Challenging, brave questions. Doubt, in this context, is a signal to listen harder.

In Oscar Trimboli's *How to Listen*[3] he discusses the 125/400 rule. We can speak 125 (to 150) words per minute, but we can listen to up to 400 words per minute. Creating a 275 word disconnect – we can listen to more than double what we can say in a minute.

Our brains are hard-wired to be super-efficient listeners, so we end up listening to the speaker and often ourselves at the same time. This is before we even start to think about the subtleties of listening to doubt. Learning to listen well, not only to the words but the tone, the emotion, and what is not being said is a super-skill and one that, regardless of the topic of doubt, has the potential to fast-track our career.

Trimboli also talks about listening for differences; this is what we are trained to do as coaches. We are hard-wired to listen for confirmation, to reaffirm our own thinking. If we can learn to listen for difference, we can listen in a way that challenges our thinking.

Three listening moves to make way for doubt

Listen for no doubt

Doubt does not always speak. Instead, it resides inside the person, struggling to articulate itself. Sometimes people feel their doubts aren't valid, or worry they'll be judged – especially if they're the only voice of dissent. This is the hazard of groupthink, where collective thinking goes unchallenged.

As a leader, listening for the absence of doubt is just as important as listening to the doubts. *No doubt is a red flag.*

How do you bring to the surface what is unspoken?

- *Role-modelling your own doubt.* Normalize it by naming your own uncertainties aloud.

- *Asking directly.* 'What are your concerns?' 'What have we not considered?'

- *Shifting the perspective.* For example, in a new product launch meeting asking the account manager, 'what do you think the retailer will push back on?' Framing it as someone's views enables it to not feel personal.

Listen for certain doubt

Doubt gets into trouble when it attracts certainty. At its core, doubt is about *uncertainty* – which in turn creates possibility. But sometimes, it becomes fused with generalization or finality.

For example: 'I doubt we'll ever deliver this project on time.' The doubt isn't the problem – it's the certainty in the word 'ever.' It shuts the door on possibility.

Another version might sound like: 'I doubt we'll ever be able to negotiate better terms with this supplier because we are a small player.' That may sound rational, but it's an unhelpful fixed belief dressed up as doubt.

How to move people forward from certain doubt:

- *With a question mark.* When you hear words like 'ever', 'never', 'can't', 'won't', attach a question mark to them – so it becomes 'ever?' The question mark invites possibility. There are always exceptions because nothing in life is certain, that is the magic.

- *Use of 'yet.'* The word 'yet' can be transformative: 'I haven't made progress… yet.' It creates forward motion and reminds us that the current state is not the final one.

- *Highlight the role of context.* Often, what feels fixed is situational. One client I worked with moved from deep frustration in June to joy in December – the only thing that changed was her new line manager and his belief in her. The doubt hadn't been wrong. It had just been locked in a false permanence.

Listen beyond the words

Listening is so much more than just hearing the words. It's tuning into the *tone, pace,* and *emotion* that sit underneath them – the *underbelly* of what's being said.

That underbelly often holds the real message: uncertainty, frustration, conviction, hesitation.

Before Teams, I coached clients almost exclusively by phone. And it worked – not despite the lack of visual cues, but *because of it.* Without the distraction of seeing someone, I found myself listening more deeply. Picking up on tiny shifts. Hearing their voice change as their thinking evolved. As Mark Nepo reflected,

> 'To listen is to lean in, softly, with a willingness to be changed by what we hear.'[4]

You don't need to be a coach to build that level of listening. But you do need to practice.

Try this: focus on just one element for a week. For example, pay attention to the tone of people's voices – not just what they're saying, but *how* they're saying it.

⊛ What do you notice? Is there a disconnect between the words and the tone? What might this be trying to tell you?

Conversation: starting to dialogue with doubt

Doubt can feel like the downer. The grit in the gears of a conversation. And yet people say they want honesty. Honesty is arguably the value which comes up most frequently in my coaching as being important to people, and it's usually in connection with the dishonesty they are experiencing. The challenge is this: honesty needs connection. That is where the role of language comes in. Language shapes our world, providing a doorway into our internal world and shaping what happens in the external world and how people react.

Think about the person in the meeting who always raises doubts. Over time, others might tune them out – not because they're wrong, but because the way the doubt is expressed can feel like friction rather than contribution. When this happens, important insights get ignored. And eventually, systemic issues emerge. If we are to lean into doubt's usefulness, then how we talk about it and how others can talk about it is vital. Often, we don't acknowledge it or at best ignore it; doubt's language needs to invite enquiry and hold no judgment. It does not act as a full stop and shut things down.

Three linguistic moves to make way for doubt

Language is how doubt gets invited in – or shut down. In this section, we explore the words and questions that help us stay open, collaborative, and constructive.

Curiosity is move one
Remember Claire Pedrick, my coaching mentor from earlier, who nicely drummed into me – 'Never ask a question you know the answer to', if you know the answer you are not engaging with doubt. Ask questions from a place of genuine curiosity, and encouragement; encouragement to explore, to go deeper and sometimes broader, to see what we can find together. It gives team members permission to relax into the not knowing, the space of doubt.

Think back to your last week of meetings. How many times did you ask a question you knew the answer to? An answer which confirmed your point of view? When I was a marketer I did this, and I suspect I am not alone in this misplaced endeavour.

Curiosity is an invitation. I like invitations, especially physical ones that you can put on your mantelpiece – the anticipation of excitement and fun that they may bring. An invitation of future possibility.

Examples of curiosity language, beyond asking questions, are:

- 'Say more': one of my favourite coaching prompts to open the door to new thinking.

- 'And?' can be a question. A heavy lifting question with power, encouraging the person to go deeper in their thinking.

The power move of 'maybe'
I love TV shows where people behave badly – ruthless, mean, self-absorbed, such as the BBC drama *Insiders* and HBO's family power struggles in *Succession*. People at their worst. The writers behind them are at their best. Nuanced, clever, and surprising. Lucy Prebble is one of the talented writers behind *Succession*. She talked about the writing team and their process:

> *'The room resonated with "maybes." Maybe this? Maybe that?*
> *Writers tend to be riddled with doubt. A trick of writing is to stay*

> *open until you absolutely have to close down the narrative, decide for sure, just so you don't miss that last possible moment of magic, that idea that solves everything. You stay alive to promise till the very last minute.*
>
> *'I remember one of the actors saying at a season one read through, how he'd never seen scripts with so many "maybes." The occasional maybe is no bad thing. It is not always uncertainty or lack of confidence. It's an offer, it's a kindness, it's a gesture to another artist: Here's how I picture it, but how do you picture it? Do you have a better idea? There's room. You are involved.'[5]*

The power of 'maybe': at last count, *Succession* has won 83 awards. 'Maybe' creates space for alternative thinking and perspectives to be shared. It's a way to introduce a different point of view and encourage others to offer their thinking too.

Examples of maybe language:

- 'Maybe it could be this?' 'Maybe it could be that?'
- 'Maybe we can talk this through some more?'
- 'Maybe we can look at some other options?'
- 'Maybe we could ask the other functions what we can do?'
- 'Maybe there are other points of view in the room we need to consider, who would like to share a different perspective?'

'Maybe' language is doubt in action. In the startup world, that might sound like: 'What if we test a minimum viable product?' or 'Let's create a few hypotheses.' These phrases don't signal indecision – they signal *openness*.

The collaborative effect of 'I don't know'

When I worked in marketing, there was a horrible process. The advertising agency would present their ideas to us, then there would be silence, before the most junior person was asked to say what they thought of the presented work. Potentially terrifying if you are that junior person. All I could ever think was, 'what if I get this wrong?'; there was no headspace for doubt. The process came from a good place: to share everyone's thinking and to not be influenced by hierarchy. But as the junior person there was not an option to say, 'I don't know', and given they had the least experience this would not have been an unreasonable response. By expressing our self-doubt, we give room for others to express their thoughts and their doubts – 'I don't know, the parts of this that I think work are... what do you think?' It can invite a team effort to create and collaborate.

The 'I' makes it a solo endeavour; changing it to 'we don't know' makes it a team endeavour; something that we must get our heads around collaboratively in order to move forward.

Examples of 'don't know' language:

* I don't know but let's look at what we do know.

* What would we do next if we did know?

* What do we need to know to help us make a decision?

* What are we assuming here?

When we change the way we talk and listen for doubt, we move from shutdown to enquiry. From hesitation to collaboration. From grit in the gears to fuel for better thinking.

In the next chapter we explore how to actively fuel the conversation and move from dialogue to decision.

Doubt distilled: six ways to steer through situational doubt

* *Doubt needs a safe place to land.* A psychologically safe space – where people feel included, encouraged, and unpunished – turns doubt from a whisper into a worthwhile signal.

- *Steer first.* Leaders go first by holding space, not giving answers. When leaders model their own doubts and ask questions they don't know the answer to, they give others permission to do the same.

- *No doubt is a red flag.* The absence of doubt isn't confidence – it might be silence, fear, or groupthink. If no one is voicing concern, the real issue might be that it doesn't feel safe to do so.

- *Certainty kills possibility.* When doubt fuses with certainty – 'we'll never', 'we can't' – progress stalls. Reframe those moments with 'yet', a question mark, or a shift in context to reopen the door to insight.

- *Language shapes the climate.* Words like *maybe, I don't know*, and *say more* create space for exploration. They turn conversations from defensive to developmental. Doubt doesn't shut the door – it holds it open.

- *Listening changes everything.* To steer through doubt, leaders must listen beyond what is said – to what's missing, what's implied, and what might be unspoken emotionally. Great listening is not passive – it's transformative.

So, after all the listening, surfacing, and exploring – what is stopping you from deciding?

Chapter 11:
The 'do' in situational doubt II: turning doubt into wiser decisions

'I realized I have never really listened fully before.' That was the brutally honest reaction of a Director during a training session I ran for senior leaders. A good sign the training was working – shifting awareness and behaviour. Unfortunately, the rest of his colleagues were also not listening to each other either, as they discussed how to create a coaching culture within their side of the business. The conversation swirled and stalled. Eventually I parked it for the day. Something needed to shift. A change of approach was required.

The next morning, I split them into two groups: one to develop the approach, the other to challenge it. Within the hour, they had landed on a clearer, sharper solution. The grain of doubt focused the collective argument, bringing new thinking and with that the ability to get to a decision.

The self-awareness, listening, and language skills already discussed make it possible for doubt to land well, and for teams to be receptive to hearing it. And tools and structure help convert that openness into movement. They are the fuel in the tank to complete the journey.

In this chapter, we will explore tools to:

1. Work through situational doubt together.

2. Activate a decision.

This chapter is a practical resource – one to dip into and return to.

Tools to work through situational doubt together

There are two sets of tools: those which help surface the doubt, and those that enable you to work through it. Firstly, surfacing doubt:

Schedule a meeting with doubt (solo or shared)

Invite doubt to a meeting – literally. The meeting can be on your own or with others. I had one client who would schedule a weekly meeting with doubt:

> *'I look at the project I'm doing, and ask myself lots of questions, and actively doubt myself: Have I really done all the research? Is there any other way? If I was someone else coming into this project, what would they say? Sometimes I think about people I worked with, for example, if my old manager was coming in, what would he say? Am I being innovative enough? Am I taking enough risk? Either good ideas come out of it, or it's reassuring to know I am on the right track.'*

The rigour of a weekly opportunity to doubt is rich with reward. Doubt challenged her repeatedly to push the boundaries and innovate.

The purpose is to interrogate, with the help of doubt, something you are working on – a project, a difficult conversation you are preparing for, even perhaps something that you do regularly and ask: is there a different way of thinking about this?

When we invite doubt into the room, it needs structure – not to control it, but to help it serve its purpose. Otherwise, doubt can meander, stall, or create discomfort. Techniques you can use to surface doubt in your meeting include:

The TACT framework
TACT gives you a four-part conversation to have – whether you are tackling a tough decision, testing a new strategy, or surfacing team concerns. TACTfully exposing the doubts that may exist.

Use each quadrant as a phase in your conversation, or as a menu of prompts to spark dialogue.

T – Talk to the missing voices
When we are lost in our own thinking, we can forget to utilize the wisdom of others – *who is not in the room and what might they say?*

- Which stakeholder's voice have we not considered and what would their feedback be?

- Whose expertise would be useful here, what would they advise?

- What would the customer feedback be on this?

- Who might disagree with us – and what might they say?

A – Ask our assumptions
When we are close to something we can become blind to our assumptions – *what might we be taking for granted?*

- What assumptions are we making here?

- What would happen if these assumptions were false?

- What might be driving our assumptions? Who might benefit from them being true?

- What are we treating as fact, which might actually be a belief?

C – Creative challenge

At the heart of the creative challenge is the goal of thinking differently. Borrow creativity from different sources – yourselves, other people, sectors, and being inspired by the constraints and limitations, to ask: *how else could we look at this?*

* If we were to come up with three alternative ways of approaching this what would they be?

* Stand in different shoes: if we were a different industry (e.g., tech, media, retail, not for profit) how would we approach this differently?

* If we had twice (or half) the resources – people, money, time – how would we approach this?

T – Time travel

The past, present, and future can bring different perspectives – *what would they say?*

* What do I know from the past, which I need to consider today?

* What is happening now that could change how I am thinking about this?

* What would the future advise me to do now?

* If this was to go brilliantly, what would I be doing right now to make that happen?

Other frameworks, such as Edward de Bono's *Six Thinking Hats*, can help us to explore different perspectives – facts, emotions, risks, possibilities. If your team is familiar with this approach, you can use the Hats to deepen one or more stages of the TACT framework.

Question-storming

A structured method that begins with doubts and helps surface the most productive ones to explore:

- *Define the challenge.* Frame it clearly – for example, 'Our customer engagement has dropped by 25%' or 'We're stuck on the next steps in the product roadmap.'

- Set a timer (10–15 minutes). *Generate as many questions as possible about the challenge* – no answers allowed. Go for volume. Aim for 30 to 50 questions, without judgment or filtering.

- *Cluster and review.* Group related questions and look for themes.

- *Choose the strongest.* Select the questions that feel most energising, disruptive, or insight-opening – and explore those further together.

Different approaches to work through and challenge the doubts:

The red team approach

The red team approach is inspired by the high-stakes world of venture capital, a world built on uncertainty. Venture capitalists hunt for the elusive unicorn to invest large sums into unproven ideas. As David Sze the venture capitalist reflected:

> 'The best early-stage venture capital investments appear obvious in retrospect; however, very few of them are actually obvious when you make them.'[1]

These Professional Doubters have a process they follow to decide on investments, and it can be applied by anyone who wants to use doubt to find the brilliance in an idea.

This research was originally summarized in the *Harvard Business Review* article 'Make Decisions with a VC Mindset' by Ilya A. Strebulaev and Alex Dang.[2] VCs question everything; they disagree wildly and often do not get to consensus. And that is ok, because collectively it allows them to get to a more informed decision.

How?

- Before deciding on a prospective investment, they gather feedback by having each person share their views independently.

- In the meeting they assign a 'red team' of people who are tasked with arguing against a deal and strengthening the idea.

- Ultimately, the person who is proposing the investment has the final say in whether they want to invest, but they have gathered all the 'doubt' to enable them to flow to a decision.

- They are not looking for consensus or the group collectively coming to one point of view; instead, the decision is ultimately made by the proposer.

This approach looks to strengthen the argument or weaken it based on the red team's doubting questions.

This same approach can work with groups where people are assigned to challenge the thinking and build on it – 'The challenge with this is… and what might make it better is…'

The conviction scale: scoring our doubt
Borrowing again from the world of venture capitalists, we can learn from the questions they ask in investment meetings:

- What is your level of conviction that we should invest in this company?

- How do you score that conviction between 1 and 10, with 1 being low and 10 high?

Conviction is interesting as it is the opposite of doubt, and by scaling our answer it allows the doubt to surface. If someone rates something an 8, those 2 missing points often hold the most revealing doubts. This gives you a doorway into understanding them, to mine and explore and see if there are any insights that would be helpful.

When coaching, I ask clients to score where they are in terms of their thinking or feelings relating to the subject, and if they answer below a 10, it's always a cue for us to probe and ask, 'what would take you to a 10?' It gives people permission to open up and to be imaginative about what the possible solutions might be. Sometimes it is easier for the person to think about what would nudge it up 1 point rather than a few points to a 10. Then, when they have made a 1-point nudge again, what would nudge it up another point and so on. Without fail, additional thinking always comes forward.

Making the counter-argument
Making the counter-argument is a good way of working with the doubts on either side of the case. This approach reduces bias, uncovers blind spots, and ensures the doubts are fully explored.

There is often a lone voice of doubt in a team, perhaps expressing concerns about the product launch, the restructure, or the reallocation of the budget. The role of the leader is to enable that voice to be heard.

Key counter-argument techniques:

1. *The 'ask doubt?' test*

   Actively explore what doubts would surface if you chose to do the opposite.

   Ask: 'What if we pursued the opposite decision or direction – what challenges would arise from that?'

2. *The strongest case against*

   Develop a compelling case for an alternative approach.

   Ask: 'What would be a compelling alternative approach? How could you make this successful?'

3. *The 'inversion' method*

   Identifies risks before they become problems.

   Instead of asking: 'What will make this successful?', ask: 'What would cause this to fail?'

Bridging to decision: the doubt bomb

One of the most powerful moves in working through situational doubt is surfacing it early. As Oscar Trimboli, author of *How to Listen*, says:

> *'If you hold a different perspective, declare it early rather than wait until the end, when your different perspective can feel like a conversational hand grenade – blowing up the progress that others feel they have made.'*[3]

This is the essence of the doubt bomb – not an explosion, but an opening. If you have concerns, voice them early, and frame them with possibility: 'I have a concern about the timings of the new product launch and whether we can create enough inventory for the launch to coincide with the marketing campaign. What if we considered alternative timings or initially launching in one format for the first six months?' Tools like this don't remove doubt – they give it a starring role. They help us move from swirling uncertainty to constructive clarity.

Tools to activate a decision

Brilliant doubt demands a decision. When a decision is absent, we are only using the side of doubt that stagnates us and the business. Often, decisions can take the form of dilemmas.

Some of the most challenging decisions which need to be made are 'either/or' decisions – dilemmas. We navigate dilemmas all day: should I go to the gym or stay home and tidy up, or should we run a two-day or one-day team-building event? Over time, we become skilled at making these choices, and the process we develop for making them is deeply furrowed into our unconscious and neural pathways. Therefore, we don't know the process we use to solve these dilemmas.

Fons Trompenaars and Charles Hampden-Turner's 'dilemma theory' looks at how to bring together what appears to be a double bind and reconcile both viewpoints to move forward. It looks at how to expose and reconsider decisions which are unconscious to find different perspectives. Hampden-Turner argues that

> 'we can never fully grow until we embrace the behaviours and attitudes that are most uncomfortable to us. The most effective management practices are those that gently force engineers, managers, and employees to embrace the unthinkable.'[4]

Progress comes from firmly standing outside our comfort zones and sitting in our self- and situational doubts. The process was shared in their 1985 report *Through the Looking Glass* (a title borrowed from the sequel to Lewis Carroll's *Alice in Wonderland*), which was written for Shell.[5] They identified an approach to help the senior leaders at Shell work through their dilemmas. Interestingly, it was only circulated internally to a very narrow senior audience. The Managing Directors were fearful of it having a wider audience, thinking that if it was known that the senior leaders had doubts their stock price would fall. Their approach is based on the principles:

- Dilemmas are not problems to be solved but paradoxes to be reconciled.

- Instead of 'either/or' thinking, it considers 'and/both' thinking to get to creative solutions which incorporate both sides.

The heart of dilemma theory is this: instead of choosing one option over the other, it asks leaders, '*How can we get the best of both?*' For example, leaders often feel forced to choose between short-term results and long-term growth. Dilemma theory reframes the question: '*What can we do to boost sales this quarter while also investing enough in product development for the future?*' The process:

- Name the extreme positions and the reasons they might make sense.

- Bring respect and not judgment to each side, regardless of your initial point of view.

- It rests on being able to see the points of view as complementary, not competing, and thinking about what connects them.

Situational doubt, when done well, doesn't slow us down – it strengthens what we build. It helps us surface what's unspoken, challenge what's assumed, and expand what's possible. These tools aren't about indulging hesitation. They're about equipping ourselves and others to move forward with clarity and care.

Try one of these tools this week. Invite a little doubt into your next meeting. Not to slow you down – but to find something better. Doubt isn't the problem. It's the partner you need.

Doubt distilled: moving from uncertainty to a decision

- *Invite doubt deliberately.* Treat doubt as a thought partner, not a saboteur. Create space – solo or shared – to ask hard questions and challenge current thinking. Scheduling time to meet with doubt gives it shape, safety, and purpose.

- *Structure the conversation for insight.* Use frameworks like TACT and question-storming to shape open exploration into targeted discovery. Doubt thrives in structure – not to tame doubt, but to aim it towards deeper understanding.

- *Challenge your conviction.* The conviction scale makes doubt visible. A missing point or two between your current conviction and a 10 holds valuable insight – what's still unresolved, what's missing, or what could change the game.

- *Build the counter-case.* Assign red teams, pose the strongest opposing argument, or explore the inversion – what could make this fail? These tools flip our mental models, revealing what we might otherwise miss or ignore.

- *Turn doubt into decision.* Doubt without decision breeds paralysis. Use the 'doubt bomb' to voice concerns early and creatively. Move from hesitation to proposal – reframing uncertainty as a starting point for action.

- *Work through the dilemma, not around it.* Situational doubt often arises from tension between two valid paths. Dilemma theory helps reframe 'either/or' as 'both/and,' inviting us to hold complexity long enough to reach wiser, more integrated choices.

But, what to do if the doubt is bigger than the situation?

*'If a man will begin with certainties, he shall
end in doubts; but if he will be content to begin
with doubts, he shall end in certainties.'*

- Francis Bacon

*part
four*

Systemic Doubt

Chapter 12:
The invisible architecture: systemic drivers of doubt

In the UK, Sir Alan Bates consistently doubted and challenged the Post Office, which had wrongly accused him and hundreds of other subpostmasters of theft. Between the late 1990s and 2010s, accounting discrepancies caused by a faulty IT system called Horizon, developed by Fujitsu, led to what is now recognized as one of the gravest miscarriages of justice in British history. Despite mounting evidence that the Fujitsu IT system was flawed, the Post Office refused to listen. Instead, it turned its doubt onto individuals, pursuing them through the courts, and resulting in many innocent people being imprisoned, rather than questioning the structure it had built its operations on.

In 2009, Bates founded the Justice for Subpostmasters Alliance (JFSA). In 2010, journalist Nick Wallis began writing extensively about what was happening. Still, the system did not listen. It reinforced its walls, defending the edifice, and focused on blame rather than repair.

The ITV drama *Mr Bates vs The Post Office* (2024) helped bring this miscarriage of justice into wider public awareness. Yet, at the time of writing, the system continues to turn its wheels slowly: many subpostmasters remain without full compensation. This was not only a failure of technology, but of leadership, of culture, and of government itself. The foundations were unsound, and the cracks in the architecture ran deep.

What this shows us is that the problem was not simply the decisions of a few individuals. It was systemic. To see why, we need to be clear about what we mean by a system.

What a system is

A system is the whole architecture within which an organization operates. It is made up of the visible structures we can point to – people, teams, reporting lines, operating models, and resources, and the less visible elements that hold them together. These include the foundations and frameworks: culture, power dynamics, assumptions, and networks of influence.

Just as a building is more than walls and windows, a system is more than its surface. Its strength and safety depend on what lies beneath: the hidden supports, wiring, and foundations that shape how the whole structure behaves. When those unseen elements are sound, the system can adapt and endure. When they are weak, faulty, or ignored, the entire structure is at risk – no matter how polished it looks on the outside.

This is the invisible architecture: the interplay of visible and invisible elements that creates outcomes no single individual intends, but which everyone inside must live with.

What systemic doubt is

When it comes to doubt, the system is often the invisible hand that either silences it or allows it to surface. In the case of the subpostmasters, their doubt in the system and the challenge they faced were clear, but the architecture they were up against had no capacity to doubt itself. The structure was too rigid, its foundations too flawed, and its defences too strong.

Systemic doubt is an organization's ability to question its own architecture – its structures, rules, and culture, rather than simply doubting individuals. Without this capacity, doubt gets misdirected, punishing the people within the structure instead of repairing the structure itself.

Systemic doubt is different from situational doubt, which can often be traced to a specific context, data point, relationship, or decision. Systemic doubt is more diffuse – part of the ether. It rises not from what is happening here and now, but from how things always seem to happen.

Some systems generate confidence. Many people educated in the UK's private school system, for example, carry a natural assurance. A 2015 study by the Centre for Learning and Life Chances in Knowledge Economies and Societies (*Dreaming Big*)[1] found that private school pupils reported higher self-esteem, a stronger sense of control, and greater access to influential networks. That confidence doesn't appear out of nowhere, it is system-fed: through opportunity, exposure, expectation, and affirmation.

But the same forces that breed confidence can also entrench certainty. Systems that reward assurance and status can become resistant to challenge, creating cultures where doubt is seen as weakness. As Margaret Heffernan reminds us in *Wilful Blindness*,[2] our brains reward us for certainty. Neuroscientists at Emory University found that when people defended tightly held beliefs, the same reward circuits lit up as when an addict gets a fix. Systems, like individuals, can become hooked on certainty and blind to doubt, even when the evidence is mounting.

In the same way, some systems generate doubt or silence, particularly in those who don't see themselves represented or valued within the structure. This is why many organizations are now interrogating their systems: acknowledging the barriers that have historically limited progress for women, people of colour, LGBTQ+ individuals, and those from lower socio-economic backgrounds. Measures like blind job applications, demographic tracking, and DEI (Diversity, Equity and Inclusion) training are not just cultural shifts, they are structural responses to systemic doubt. Doubt that says: maybe this system isn't working equally for everyone.

The invisible architecture of the system

What is this invisible system? Let's start with what is visible – the person. Self-doubt resides within the individual: am I good enough? Surrounding the person is situational doubt – the room they are in, the carpet, the walls and furniture, prompting them to wonder: what is going on here? Beyond this is systemic doubt, the unseen infrastructure that connects the individual to the wider world, prompting the deeper question: why does this always happen?

The visible consequences of unspoken doubt

When systems discourage challenge, doubt doesn't vanish – it simply goes unspoken. It's still present, but it lives in whispers, in private frustrations, in the quiet decisions people make to disengage. Over time, this silence carries a heavy cost.

In *Careless People: A Story of Where I Used to Work*, Sarah Wynn-Williams[3] describes how, in 2014, Mark Zuckerberg was issued with an arrest warrant in South Korea. Obviously not good – especially when Facebook (now Meta) was trying to break into the Korean market. A visit was planned, but there was a snag: Zuckerberg, understandably, didn't want to be arrested. At a high-level meeting, they started strategizing. The idea surfaced – send someone else ahead of Mark to see if they get arrested first. A kind of 'test-the-waters' arrest strategy.

As they went around the table, each executive subtly dodged the 'bullet' until Sarah Wynn-Williams, then Director of Public Policy, had a slow, chilling realization: 'I'm to be the sitting target.'

She's the one they think should go.

She's the one they're willing to risk.

Let that land: the company you work for is casually considering sending you to a country where you might be arrested – just to see what happens. This isn't a request to work late. This is asking you to risk your freedom.

No one at the table challenged the idea.

No one said: 'Wait – is this okay?'

No doubts were raised.

Sarah describes a culture where dissent was not wanted – where concerns were met at best with indifference, at worst with hostility. Over time, people stopped speaking up. Not because they stopped seeing, but because it had become clear: there was no point.

Doubt was still present, but it went underground.

Whether it was letting Zuckerberg win when playing a board game, not telling Sheryl Sandberg, Zuckerberg's number two, the real reason Angela Merkel refused to meet, or downplaying Facebook's role in the rise in hate speech in Myanmar, the system stopped listening to doubt. Doubt had gone into hiding. And without systemic doubt, the checks and balances were missing. The culture became doubt-free not because no one saw it, but because no one felt safe enough to say it.

When doubt hides in the system, we may experience:

- *Loud optimism.* When everyone has drunk the Kool-Aid. People high on positivity and groupthink prevails. Action and momentum to move forward, captured by the spirit of 'Move fast and break things'.

- *Quiet rumblings.* When concerns are quietly voiced in corridor conversations, but not to the people who need to hear them. The rumblings of cynicism – 'despite not delivering he always manages to get promoted.'

- *Silo conversations.* Pockets where doubt resides but doesn't connect outside the silo.

- *Silence.* Keep quiet and carry on. People sense and know that speaking out will make no difference, so they quieten their doubts. They may have seen what has happened to their colleagues when they speak out and know that keeping quiet is the best way forward. A learned helplessness occurs.

What happened at Facebook was a systemic failure. The system did not structurally protect dissenting voices. There were no feedback loops built into its governance that allowed challenge to rise and be heard. The result? When the 'test-the-waters arrest strategy' was floated, no one said, 'This is mad.' And that, in itself, is mad.

Decision-making was centralized at the top with Zuckerberg and Sandberg, but accountability was pushed down. Those with less power were considered expendable. That's what ultimately happened to Sarah Wynn-Williams: by the end of the book she is asked to leave. For her, the lack of systemic doubt pushed the stakes too high.

These systemic dynamics produced a culture of compliance and silence, where senior leaders were not questioned even when decisions were ethically or personally dangerous. *Doubt became a private emotion, not a shared conversation.* Over time, people stopped speaking up not because they didn't care, but because they saw that nothing changed.

In my work with teams, I often see the same pattern: they voice concerns, raise doubts, suggest improvements, yet nothing shifts. Eventually, they stop engaging. Not because they've stopped thinking, but because the system has stopped listening.

Culture is how people behave; systems are what shape those behaviours. A culture of silence can only persist when the system rewards compliance and punishes challenge. When no one speaks up, it's rarely just fear or apathy – it's about the consequences the system enforces, and the signals it sends.

This is where Otto Scharmer's concept of *absencing* offers insight. In his book *The Essentials of Theory U* (2018),[4] he discusses how absencing refers to a state where individuals or systems disconnect from their environment, leading to destructive patterns of behaviour. The absencing occurs when individuals or systems:

- *Close their minds.* Ignore or dismiss doubts raised or data which may contradict the plan.

- *Close their hearts.* A lack of empathy and disconnect from others – it was ok for Wynn-Williams to possibly face jail to test the waters with Korea.

- *Close their will.* Avoid action, change or accountability.

Scharmer's model shows this as a cycle of denying, 'de-sensing,' blaming, and ultimately destruction. A collective denial about seeing what is really going on. When systems are in a state of absencing they literally can't hear or hold systemic doubt, so it gets buried. Systemic doubt is a healthy signal – it is the systems trying to wake up, rather than be asleep, it is shining a light on what needs to be listened to.

The drivers of systemic doubt

We need to stop any potential 'organ rejection,' said the Chief Executive. The 'organs' were two newly appointed directors about to join her executive leadership team. The potential 'rejectors'? The rest of the established exec team. Together they were about to embark on leading a big transformation programme in this well-known household name. Her phrase was vivid and more importantly driven by foresight and doubt. An awareness of systemic doubt.

Through the process of change there was a chance that the system would resist and 'throw out' the new starters; those who didn't have the history, the context, or the relationships, but perhaps had both the ambition to meet the new challenge and the insight to see how the system needed to be rewired. But there was a high chance the system would reject them. It might look like it was their colleagues, who are the tangible visible elements of the system, were doing the rejecting. But the reality of the system would be thornier and more knotted than that.

Understanding the interconnectedness of systems allows for their rewiring where appropriate to deliver. This Chief Executive's systemic doubt was not a flaw. She had the foresight to safeguard future work from any potential organ rejection.

To understand the role of doubt in systems, we must first notice it and observe how it interacts with and impacts on the system. Donella Meadows' work identified 12 key system levers that drive how systems operate. We will focus on the four most relevant to doubt. These are:

1. *What are the connections that fuel or weaken doubts?*

   These are the entanglements and flows between different elements – the communication channels, structure, and decision-making channels. Doubt thrives or withers based on the flow. Imagine, if there were no Slack or Teams, how it would further exacerbate the 'working from home or in the office' doubts. When the interconnections weaken, break down or are misaligned, doubt appears and trust breaks down. Take something as simple as a weekly project report. If it does not contain all the information that the leader needs to share with their key stakeholders, doubt creeps in about the project's progress. The status becomes unclear, weakens trust in the project and raises questions.

   But doubt here is a gift. It flags the issue before it breaks. If the report is not as complete as it needs to be, then if this is noticed earlier, it can lead to stronger communication, based on the needs of the recipient. It helps to further develop the author and their skills.

   Barry Oshry's[5] work on role-based pressures can be useful when thinking about the interconnections. He identifies roles at the Top, Middle, and Bottom of the organization, which helps explain why doubt can feel so different depending on your position in the system. Those at the Top may doubt whether others are able to deliver their vision and feel burdened and isolated with the responsibility. The Middles feel torn between the needs of the Tops and the Bottoms. The Bottoms may doubt they have the resources and time to make the changes. This creates three often disconnected levels, where doubts are unspoken because the system reinforces role-based blindness. This is why it often feels personal, and yet it rarely is – people question each other rather than the role the system has to play in it.

2. *How is the reality of the business aligned to its stated purpose?*

Many companies' websites state their company purpose and reason for being. In systems thinking, purpose is inferred from the company's behaviour, by what they do and not only by what they write. When behaviour and words are disconnected it creates doubt in the system. For example, on its website, Amazon states: 'We strive to be Earth's most customer-centric company, Earth's best employer, and Earth's safest place to work.' Every time they are in the news about employee challenges, this is thrown into question. In December 2024, Amazon mandated a full-time return to the office for its corporate employees. The strikes and unionization challenges are well reported. This might raise doubts for some: do they want to join this kind of organization? It enables the person to make an informed decision as to whether they are right to work for this company or not, whether it aligns with their values.

3. *How well are we listening and responding to doubts?*

The way a system listens and responds is through its feedback loops. The mechanisms it uses to learn and adapt to new and or changing knowledge. They are deeply connected to doubt, because the system's ability to respond to feedback will either enable it to build trust or to weaken it. A healthy system listens to the signals, including the whispers of doubt and dissent, and responds. A healthy system leans into the brilliance that can be found in doubt to future-proof itself. However, when it ignores the issues, the doubt can grow. Or if it is inconsistent in its approach it can confuse people and cause them to falter.

A positive feedback loop might be when a person receives an unexpected email from a director, congratulating them on some work and explaining the impact of it on the business. Boosting morale and reinforcing behaviours has a halo effect on their colleagues who see good performance being recognized by their senior leaders. In contrast, a negative feedback loop can degrade trust quickly. Like when one of my clients received a phone call on Christmas Day to discuss a work project. I don't need to spell out the impact that had on my client, who was surrounded by her small children at that time. That said, I would not have been surrounded by small children, and my anger would have been equally high. The system in that moment sent a loud signal: boundaries are not going to be respected here, at any time.

4. *What are the written and unwritten rules for how we get things done here?*

The policies, stated practices, and the informal 'this is the way it's done here' all shape the system. Rules signal what the system values. They also show what people will be rewarded for. Rewards are a signal of what the system appreciates and responds well to. Rules whereby there is a lack of consistency between stated values and actual behaviours will erode belief in the system itself, casting doubt on it.

'The greatest leverage of all is to keep oneself unattached... to stay flexible, to realize that no paradigm is "true" – just useful. And to be willing to let go of assumptions and embrace new ones.'[6]

To be able to see a system, we need to look beneath the surface and know that what we may be looking at in one point in time may change our interpretation of it in that moment. It is only an interpretation and not the truth. The brilliance of doubt is that it allows the holder to look at the system in a different way – to detach from what we think is known, and to see different attachments and connections to what was there before. Organizations that can say 'we were wrong' or 'we need to rethink everything' invite courage instead of cynicism.

Doubt has the potential to create healthy systems.

And healthy systems have the power to create doubt.

A circular strength – each one making the other better.

Doubt distilled: the invisible architecture

- *Systemic doubt isn't personal – it's structural.* It rises from the values, incentives, and patterns that quietly shape what's normal, rewarded, or ignored.

- *When purpose and practice don't align, doubt grows.* A bold mission means nothing if the system rewards the opposite. Doubt surfaces in the space between the two.

- *Silence doesn't mean there's no doubt – it means doubt isn't safe.* People still notice. They've just learned it's wiser not to speak.

- *Feedback loops make or break trust.* In healthy systems, doubt is heard and acted on. In unhealthy ones, it's ignored until it festers underground.

- *The rules – written and unwritten – reveal what the system protects.* Who gets promoted, who gets punished, what gets praised: these are doubt's real signals.

- *Paradigms shape what gets questioned and what gets defended.* Doubt challenges the myths we've mistaken for truth, and asks: is this still the system we want to belong to?

What do we have to gain from encouraging doubt in a system?

Chapter 13:
When the system is not brilliant: the power in doubt

My client had doubts about whether she should stay in her organization. She described feeling discombobulated and close to burnout. She had a young son and was keen to have a second. On the surface it appeared that this was about her moving into the next chapter of her life as a mum, and less about her career.

As we unpacked the discombobulation, it became clear this was not about her role as a mum. It was about the system, and what the system had asked her to do in the pandemic, which was at odds with her purpose and why she had initially chosen to do a public service role. The source of her discombobulation was coming from policy decisions that she had been part of; decisions which had impacted some vulnerable people. She had a deep discomfort about this.

At first, it felt personal. But it rarely is. We mistake systems for people. They are not the same. Yes, systems breathe through the people within them. But they are not the people. The people may change, but the system continues as it is – until, that is, it is challenged. And that is when the voice of doubt is raised.

This wasn't about a failure of resilience or a lack of commitment. She was experiencing what happens when the system asks people to carry out actions that clash with their conscience, without space for dialogue or challenge. The system was silencing the discomfort instead of listening to it.

This wasn't a personal problem – it was a systemic one. And until the system could hold space for that doubt, the cost would be borne individually, through disengagement, burnout, or exit.

For my client, the answer lay in the awareness of what was driving her thinking, by being aware that she could challenge and raise her doubts. With this insight, she proactively followed through with conversations with key people. There were some challenging conversations and moments of truth shared on both sides. What kept her there was the reconnection to her purpose and truly believing that she could make a difference for the community.

This chapter focuses on the brilliance of systemic doubt and why it matters whether doubt is heard or silenced. Systems do not question themselves and without being questioned they don't learn or evolve. Instead, they defend, stay silent, and blame others. And the cost of that silence is high.

Doubt needs agency. It needs voice. That is where Professional Doubt and specifically systemic doubt comes in – the practice of speaking up, asking the difficult questions, and holding a mirror up to the system. Systemic doubt is the environment. Active Doubt is the doing. Together, they can create meaningful change.

Why does systemic doubt matter?

Doubt helps us stop the blame

In 1978, United Airlines Flight 173 ran out of fuel and crashed whilst the crew were focused on resolving a landing gear issue. Despite multiple signs and warnings from the flight engineer and first officer about the dire low fuel situation, the captain failed to act on them. Ten people died. The devastating consequences of warnings being ignored.

General Stanley McChrystal discussed the crash in his book *Team of Teams: New Rules of Engagement for a Complex World.*[1]

Systemic doubt is the environment. Active Doubt is the doing. Together, they can create meaningful change.

At first glance this looks like a problem with the captain, who simply didn't listen to his crew. It would have been easy to blame him.

However, why did he not hear the warnings? The system had switched the volume off. The captain did not stand a chance of hearing them. Why?

The cockpit was organized around a rigid hierarchy. The captain held ultimate authority, and the team around him were discouraged from questioning him. The system suppressed the doubt from other crew members even when the stakes were life or death. The first officer and the flight engineer did raise their concerns with the captain, but they were not heard or acted upon. The culture in the system meant their voices were not taken seriously, and there was no way of elevating their concerns. Everyone was focused on the immediate problem of the gear issue; the system didn't make space for new information to be considered and incorporated into its latest thinking. There was no flexibility or adaptability.

This tragedy led to the development of Crew Resource Management (CRM) – a systemic transformation which baked in doubt as a vital tool for safety in the industry. CRM is a training framework which embeds shared responsibility, open communication, and mutual respect across all flight crew members. Doubt is proactively encouraged – team members are to speak up, challenge, and collaboratively reassess situations. Over time, CRM has evolved beyond a technical procedure into a cultural shift.

Without systemic doubt, systems fail.

Without Professional Doubt, people help those systems to fail.

Sometimes fatally.

However, CRM shows what can happen when doubt is given not just a voice, but a structure.

We no longer misdirect our blame at each other. We stop questioning people's ability or intent and instead ask, 'what is it in the system that has shaped their behaviour?' We are not looking to address the symptom but the root cause.

Barry Oshry's work is grounded in this truth: people behave not because of who they are, but because of where they are in the system. When we are blind to the system, we project its pressures onto each other. We blame each other, instead of seeing that it is the system that is in the driving seat.

It is not personal, and yet how many times do we blame each other for what is going wrong at work? This is why we need to give doubt a voice and a place. Not to weaken doubt, but to wake it up. To start looking clearly at the system.

The system cannot see itself; doubt is the mirror.

The mirror that shows a new perspective, an often-missed perspective. A perspective that can change everything.

'It is just the way it is here.' 'What can I do?' The cries of learned helplessness. This is what happens when we are caught on the treadmill of the system, putting one foot in front of the other and not going anywhere. We feel we cannot effect change and become passive actors. A couple of times I have been briefed by a leadership team who want to empower the teams below them to take more proactive action. These groups are what Barry Oshry would call the Middles, and they can often feel like all their agency has been squeezed out of them. The conversation often goes along the lines of: how can we upskill them? Have we got the right people at this level? Instead, I redirect them to: what is it in the system that is driving this behaviour? For example, what are the structures and processes that stop the team stepping up? How does the system reward or punish team behaviour and output?

Too often, organizations treat doubt as a people problem, assuming the challenge is with the person, when in fact it points to a systemic issue. Professional Doubt helps us to recognize that signal and respond constructively.

Action happens when we come together, but the absence of partnership across the system creates silos, where each section is working for their own silo and is not connecting for the greater good. Siloed doubt stays stuck. Silos are common in organizations, and some of the biggest can be found in Mergers & Acquisitions. PWC, for example, was used to being the advisor. They found themselves switching roles to being the acquired, when in 2002 they were bought for £3.5 billion by IBM. Two giant silos needing to come together to work as one. When an IBMer was asked what he would do differently next time he was in this situation, he reflected: 'I would really trust the other side more.' He realized that Professional Doubt is most powerful when turned inward – allowing him to question the 'false truths' his own side had assumed.

By ignoring systemic doubt, we are giving up on the system's chance to learn, to innovate.

We put the system on hold.

Active Doubt agitates. It breaks the cycle. It dismantles silos.

By shifting our focus from the person to the system, we unlock the brilliance sitting inside systemic doubt. It does not just hold the mirror – it shows us the risks we might otherwise miss.

Doubt is the risk radar

Systemic doubt is both our risk radar and our ethical governor. It signals when something is off, but also ensures that the questions of fairness, accountability, and trust are not lost in the rush to act.

I coached someone who worked in finance in the City. It was not a typical brief. He was doing well, and he kept moving organizations, but the reason he moved was because he kept finding himself in positions where things were going wrong. There was some level of questionable behaviour that needed to be flagged to his seniors. He was becoming the serial whistle-blower. He wanted to understand: why him? Why did he keep finding himself these situations? And why did he feel compelled to speak up?

Whistle-blowers can see the system; they act by holding the mirror back up to it – even when the system looks away. Often the system doesn't want to look at itself, as in the case of my client, who ended up leaving his organization because questions were left unanswered. He was uncomfortable with what was happening. The system was protecting the silence.

Why was he so good at seeing what others didn't? We discovered it was his upbringing that compelled him to speak out, the way he had been raised by his family with a strong moral compass. In the playground, if he saw someone being bullied, he was the one who would step in and stop it. This, combined with his personality type, meant that he was hard-wired to speak truth to power because of his internal motivations. Maybe others saw it too – but they chose to turn a blind eye. He couldn't. He had to speak up. Systemic doubt often starts as individual unease. But when no one else names it, the one who does becomes a threat to the system's comfort zone.

What was special about my client was his doubt detection skills. Some people are especially attuned to doubt detection – they sense friction in the system before others even notice it. They have an ability to see the system in 3D – wide and deep. A skill that can be vital to an organization's success and mitigation of risk. A skill which we all need to develop.

Whistle-blowing originates from the literal act of blowing a whistle to alert others to something; whether on a sports pitch when the game needs to stop because of a foul, or historically when a policeman would blow their whistle to raise the alarm. Whistle-blowers put their neck on the line to alert and to warn others. But is this really the role of a few? Or is it the work of systemic doubt – part of the wider practice of Professional Doubt? If we encouraged doubt detection from all, how much healthier would our systems be? Systemic doubt, practised professionally, simply equals data. Not drama.

Drama brings a cost. And silence brings a cost too.

As we embrace artificial intelligence, doubt becomes a quality we need to maximize its potential. Reid Hoffman, in *Superagency: What Could Possibly Go Right with Our AI Future*,[2] describes AI as a 'huge intelligence amplifier' – a tool that can expand human agency, creativity, and productivity rather than replace us. But amplification only works if humans define our role in shaping it. We must design the systems around AI, not let AI's systems design us.

This is where doubt matters. I sometimes find myself 'arguing' with AI. It speaks with absolute confidence, and often it is right, but sometimes it isn't. That certainty can seduce us into passivity. Being willing to challenge it is vital. Today's systems, trained on incomplete or biased data, are already embedded in our decision-making. They are fusing together at speed, often invisibly, and raising urgent ethical questions about how data is used, how intellectual property is protected, and who benefits. AI is fusing together across businesses, industries and society, creating interlocking systems which can benefit but also distort. The risk is not only technical error, but moral complacency. Our role here is to be the champion of doubt – to test, to build guard rails, to ensure it is working for us, for the betterment of organizations and society at large.

Doubt must be our ethical governor. Not to slow innovation for its own sake, but to ensure we ask the questions that matter: who benefits? Who is harmed? What don't we know? How is this in line with our purpose and values? Systemic doubt is not a luxury here; it is a systemic safeguard for fairness, accountability, and trust. As Hoffman himself argues, the future demands 'smart risk-taking',[3] with the smartness coming from iterative deployment, feedback loops, and regulation that enables innovation without blinding us to its consequences. There are plenty of doomsayers with AI, but doubt brings hope with it. It brings the very human qualities of critical thinking, ethics, and principles that need to be interwoven into the models.

The future demands doubt to step up; for it to become ever more active and present in how organizations build their AI capabilities and offers. Without it, we are open to greater risks. With it, AI can create untold benefit for us and not the other way round.

Doubt is the agent of change

Systemic doubt is the mirror which prompts change. The system cannot change without looking at itself clearly in the mirror first. Then it must act.

Active Doubt is the disruptor of stuck patterns and inertia. It can give agency to the organization, by asking: does it have to be this way? It invites action and not just reflection.

But action is hard. People are immune to change, as are systems. Kegan and Lahey developed their Immunity to Change framework[4] to explain how we can be committed to change whilst at the same time unconsciously defending against it happening. At the heart of their idea is the notion of hidden competing commitments, which the system (and the people) are unconsciously trying to protect.

When an organization says, 'We are committed to investing in our talent', the competing commitment might be, 'Our shareholders' expectations of their return; or the investment required to fund the new innovation pipeline.'

There are different drivers within the system competing for limited resources. When change doesn't happen, we often assume it's because people don't care – the classic 'blame game.' But systems theory shows it's more complex than that: resistance can stem from structural tensions, competing priorities, or feedback loops that reinforce the status quo. In other words, it's not just about people's attitudes, but about how the system itself is wired.

Systemic doubt can help surface these tensions. It lets us ask the system: what is it holding onto? What is the cost? And are we ready to challenge what we are protecting to move us forward?

Brilliant doubter: Mike, Chief Technology Officer

'Last man standing' was the nickname I had for one of my clients. We had worked through some challenging times together – when we first met, he was at risk of being let go. But a few years later, he had turned things around to such an extent that he was being considered for a global group role. It was a brutal, high-pressure business, and most of his peers had been let go in the intervening years. But there he was, still standing. It was a tough place, but he was a joy to coach.

One time, we were sat in his office. He had a fast, spider-like brain and was scribbling ideas across a whiteboard while we tried to make sense of some recent feedback. The CFO had told him he had come across as defensive in a meeting. At first glance, it looked personal. But that didn't stack up – he was one of the most humble, respectful leaders I knew. Something else was going on.

As we mapped out the system – stakeholders, functions, and current pressures – the insight emerged: the feedback wasn't about him. It was about the board's rising anxiety around a high-risk innovation project, compounded by growing financial tension. But instead of expressing that anxiety directly, the system rerouted it through individual feedback, with the CFO as the conduit. The organization lacked the language or structure to surface doubt systemically – so it showed up in coded, personal terms. As he later reflected:

'I realized I was splitting myself into two: me (the personal self) and the CTO (the role). About 80% of what I received was directed at the CTO role, and only about 20% at me as a person. Decoupling the CTO persona from the personal self became crucial. The CTO's doubt was really the organization's – a reflection of its operating model, culture, pace, and dynamics. When I doubted as a person, that was different: it reflected my fears, my willingness to stay or go, my career, my family. But most of what looked like mine actually belonged to the system?

Once he saw that, he stopped internalizing the critique and started connecting the dots across the system. He changed how he communicated the innovation story – linking it directly to the board's deeper concerns.

What had looked like his own personal defensiveness was actually the system's unspoken anxiety. The doubt wasn't personal – it was professional.

He used Professional Doubt, and specifically systemic doubt, in this case, to find his next action. And while Professional Doubt may start with the individual, it becomes transformational when it's shared. When doubt becomes a systemic practice – not just a personal act – it can change everything.

This is the flow of systemic doubt:

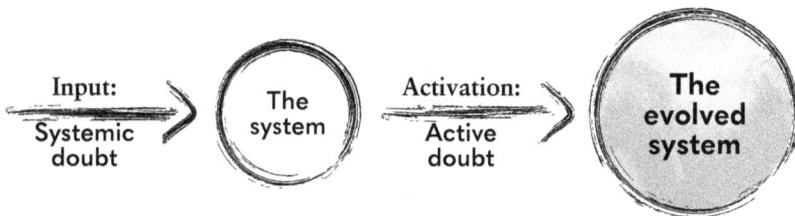

Figure 9: The flow of systemic doubt

This flow of doubt – systemic to active to evolved – is the arc we need to embed in our organizations. Systemic doubt holds up a mirror to the system and asks it to change. When it is absent, blame replaces accountability. Consequences escalate. But when Professional Doubt is present, it becomes the force that keeps systems honest, adaptive, and striving for better.

Consider:

- Where in your system is doubt being silenced?
- What is the risk of this silence?
- Who are your 'Professional Doubters'?
- What might shift if you chose to listen to them?

Doubt distilled: giving a voice to the system

- *Doubt is the system's mirror – without it, blind spots remain hidden.* Systems cannot reflect on themselves. Professional Doubt illuminates what the system misses – risks, contradictions, and unintended consequences.

- *Without Professional Doubt, inertia wins.* Systemic doubt exposes where things are stuck; Professional Doubt is the human disruption that moves them. Without it, patterns repeat and systems stagnate.

- *Blame is a smokescreen – doubt reveals the real driver.* We often blame people for problems that are systemic. Professional Doubt redirects the spotlight to structural causes, not personal failings.

- *Doubt is not a threat – it's a vital early warning system.* Professional Doubt picks up signals – discomfort, tension, friction – that precede failure. It turns vague unease into actionable insight.

* *Change doesn't happen unless the system sees what it's defending.* Systems resist change to protect what they value, often unconsciously. Professional Doubt surfaces those hidden commitments and asks what they're costing.

* *Don't leave doubt to the brave few – build it into the culture.* Healthy systems don't silence doubt or outsource it to whistle-blowers. They create space for doubt to be shared, heard, and acted upon – together.

Systemic doubt matters, it requires courage from leaders: how can we get the system to wake up and listen?

Chapter 14:
The 'do' in systemic doubt: good trouble

'You have to make good trouble.'

—John Lewis, American Civil Rights Leader and US Congressman

'Good trouble' was the embodiment of John Lewis – his entire life was devoted to standing up against injustice. At just 23 years old he was the youngest speaker at the March on Washington for Jobs and Freedom (1963), where Dr Martin Luther King Jr delivered his famous 'I Have a Dream' speech. Lewis, for over 30 years, was known as the 'conscience of the Congress', persistently and persuasively campaigning for human rights, healthcare reform, and gun control.

Good trouble is doubt with purpose – the sleeves-rolled-up version of Active Doubt. Whether the issues are deep-rooted in society or embedded in the organizations we lead, good trouble begins with the belief that systems can do better – if we ask the hard questions.

Good trouble is the embodiment and practice of Active Doubt. Active Doubt, like good trouble, drives change.

Systems don't naturally invite doubt to the table. In fact, they can actively guard against it. But we can design mechanisms to encourage and support it and, importantly, support the people who bring it. As Lewis told the Harvard graduates of 2018:

> *'Go out there. Be bold. Be courageous. Stand up. Speak up. Speak out. Get in the way. Get in good trouble, necessary trouble.'*[1]

This chapter is about how we can make the space for Active Doubt in our organizational systems. How we design the behaviours and mechanisms to enable doubt to be raised and heard. How we ensure that doubt is not punished but rewarded, and above all make doubt the active force for change that it can be.

John Lewis gave us the heartbeat of good trouble. But what does good trouble look like inside a business? Netflix offers one example. As co-founder Reed Hastings put it, 'to disagree silently is disloyal', and I would add: to disagree openly is loyal. But open dissent has to be purposeful – not grumbling to the parts of the organization that will listen, but speaking up where it can drive change. Openness with purpose is critical if doubt is to move the system forward.

In 2020, Hastings announced that he would share his CEO role with Ted Sarandos, becoming co-CEOs. This arrangement evolved further in 2023, when Greg Peters replaced Hastings as co-CEO with Sarandos, demonstrating that the model was working. The company numbers support this, with the first quarter of 2025 earnings surpassing analyst expectations with $10.54 billion revenue. A successful partnership. Much has been written about Netflix's culture, and whilst they don't make explicit reference to doubt, they imply its importance through their culture memo. Netflix has institutionalized doubt by asking employees to:

- *Say what you really think.* People are expected to question, even to challenge leaders' decisions.

- *Informed captaincy.* They have a decentralized decision model where leaders ('the captains') make decisions but with feedback and challenge from others.

- *Dream big but check yourself.* Big ambitions with a request to check yourself, as an invitation for doubt and pragmatism.

- *Is what you are doing still the right thing?* The need to constantly re-evaluate.

To disagree openly is loyal

They have created a systemic architecture that rewards doubt as a fuel for performance. They have operationalized doubt without labelling it as such. This is exemplified by the many times Sarandos has gone on record talking openly about mistakes and transparency – role-modelling Professional Doubt.

There are three ways to make doubt active in the system:

1. *Build*: design the architecture for doubt.

2. *Embed*: operationalize Active Doubt in culture.

3. *Sustain:* tune into organizational signals.

Build ══⟩ **Embed** ══⟩ **Sustain**

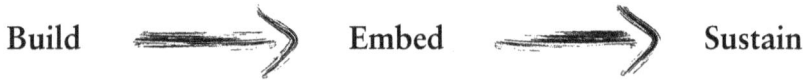

Figure 10: Build – Embed – Sustain

Systems do not naturally create the scaffolding for doubt to be useful. If we want doubt to play its role, we must design intentional structures and pathways for it to come through. Culture then provides the motivation and lived experience – the conditions that determine whether people feel able to surface their concerns or whether they keep them hidden. And this is not a one-off task. A system does not become 'good' simply because it has been designed once. Doubt must be paid attention to, actively engaged with, and continually sustained if it is to remain alive in the system.

Build: design the architecture for doubt

To activate doubt, we need to put in place the structures and places to channel it, and find the people who are willing to allow constructive debate to thrive in the system.

Structure doubt into leadership

Structure provides the formal containers for doubt to be aired. It signals to the rest of the organization the spaces where challenge is welcomed. The signal needs to start at the top: if the most senior roles create space for constructive doubt, it cascades through the culture.

Co-CEOs

A co-CEO model, like at Netflix, with clear distinctions between responsibilities, can create a healthy tension to help lead the business forward. Tension creates constructive challenge. Given the level of complexity and change that leaders are navigating now, two heads are arguably better than one.

In fact, research by Marc A. Feigen, Michael Jenkins, and Anton Warendh[2] found that the 87 public companies who had co-CEOs generated an average annual shareholder return of 9.5% – significantly better than the average of 6.9% for each company's relevant index, with 60% of companies led by co-CEOs outperforming the others. They identified factors which set up this partnership for success: complementary skills, clear responsibility, and a mechanism for conflict resolution. This is about how co-CEOs manage their respective egos and bring openness and honesty to the position as well as about parity.

The guardian of Active Doubt: the board

One of the board's primary roles is to be the guardian of Active Doubt. This is not about becoming aggressive challengers or passive rubber-stampers. The proactive guardian of doubt strikes a balance. The best boards foster enquiry, explore disagreement, and demand better thinking. The board partners as a guardian – caring for the whole system, not just the part that they are directly responsible for. They hold the different layers of the system in their hands; they are able to see the connections, the tensions, and the places where doubt needs to be heard.

Mechanisms to support the board being the guardian of Active Doubt include the following: tools for introversion and tough questions before things go wrong.

Devil's advocacy	Assigning a board member to intentionally challenge proposals to strengthen decision-making.
Pre-mortem analysis	Assessing how projects and decisions can fail or backfire before they are green-lit. This process helps identify risks and puts proactive contingency plans in place.

Codify doubt into processes

Processes are the codified channels that make it safe and possible for doubt to speak up. They allow and welcome a two-way flow of communication. Some of the clearest examples of processes come not from corporate settings, but from places where doubt can literally save lives.

Take the story of Martha Mills. In 2021, Martha died after developing sepsis at King's College Hospital, London, following a cycling accident. Her mother raised concerns about her deterioration – but those concerns were not acted upon. A coroner later ruled that Martha would most likely have survived had she been moved to intensive care earlier. If her doubt had been heard, her life might have been saved.

Martha's family have since campaigned for 'Martha's Law' – a formal right for patients and families to request a second opinion. Piloted in England and concluded in March 2025, the initiative gives patients and families 24/7 access to a second clinical review by a senior, independent critical care team if concerns are being dismissed. Staff can also trigger the process. In its first phase alone, over 2,000 calls were made, resulting in more than 300 care improvements and over 100 patients being escalated to intensive care.

Martha's Law is systemic doubt made real – a codified, designed pathway for concern to challenge authority. It's a reminder that sometimes we don't need to fix people; we need to fix processes so that people can speak and be heard.

Where might your organization need a Martha's Law? What are the red flag moments that currently have no route to escalate, challenge, or check?

Not every system needs a legal framework, but every system needs a mechanism for challenge. Many organizations are experimenting with ways to structure upward feedback and challenge – through fireside chats, informal breakfasts, rotating 'challenger panels,' or employee board representatives. The structure matters less than the intent: to create space where doubt can emerge safely, without penalty.

Formality helps. When doubt is built into processes – not just encouraged in principle – it becomes easier to surface, track, and act on. Organizations should ask:

- Where does doubt live now?
- Where does it need to live?
- What systems will help it speak?

Hire for the sweet spot of doubt

With the structure and processes in place, we need to hire for it – finding the brilliant doubters who know they're not the finished article and who stay curious. Those who are motivated by improving the system, not just navigating its power or politics. Every system comes with embedded power dynamics – that's inevitable. But they can't be the primary lever for how someone leads.

Jeremy Borys, Chief Talent Officer at Alix Partners, describes this as hiring for the 'sweet spot of doubt':

> *'I must have done over 800 interviews recruiting for Partners. When someone comes in who is overly confident – assuming they already know the culture, the business and that their past success*

will transfer seamlessly – and I don't hear doubt or wonder, I am concerned. Too much doubt can be problematic, but there is a sweet spot in the middle.'

To support the recruitment process Alix Partners uses cognitive and personality profiling assessments. The cognitive tools assess the candidates both under time pressure, and without the pressure of time. Three archetypes emerge:

- *The high-speed high-certainty type.* Who score in the top percentiles and are super smart under pressure. Some in this group are brilliant, but also overconfident in their assumptions and believe they always have the right answer.

- *The near-perfect but reflective type.* Who score slightly lower under pressure (around the top decile), and when given time, they pause, double-check, and invite input. People in this group tend to display more openness to ideas, vulnerability, patience, and discernment – 'let me double check, let me get input.'

- *Less cognitively agile.* Who score lower across both tests and are less likely to succeed in intellectually demanding environments like consultancy.

'That little sliver of uncertainty? That is where the leadership potential lives,' Borys explains. 'It is the ones who wonder, "Did I get it right?" who check their assumptions and bring others in.'

We can't test everyone like this – but we can interview for it. Adding doubt-inspired questions to the interview process helps surface this kind of thinking.

Ask questions such as:

- Tell me a time when you had doubts about a project's direction. How did you explore whether it was a personal concern or a systemic one?

- Tell me about a time when you led an initiative and encountered resistance. What did you learn about the system through that resistance?

- Tell me about a time when you influenced the culture of an organization. What structures or behaviours did you target and why?

- How have your doubts helped you lead change across a system or team?

- How do you work with others' doubts, especially when they are mirroring patterns in the wider organizations?

- What doubts do you have about this role and/or organization?

The gold we are mining for is the willingness to know they are not the finished article, and the insight that doubt can be a signal from the system, not a flaw in the person. The red flags? Over-confidence and certainty. Intellectual brilliance can be a solo sport. But most roles require collective brilliance, a team sport of many. We are looking for the green flags of a growth mindset. A brilliant doubter.

Embed: operationalize Active Doubt in culture

Systems are built and shaped by leaders who have the courage to demand a healthier system. But to make demands on the system, we need to be willing to make demands on ourselves. Or put another way, we need to turn 'good trouble' towards ourselves. Why? When leaders publicly question and actively work through those questions, they shift this as a behavioural norm across the whole system. How?

The leader eats first

Forget 'the leader eats last.' In the world of doubt, the leader eats first. First to role-model the behaviour. First to question certainty. First to demand more of the system. Leaders hold the levers of systemic change.

This early, visible engagement with uncertainty is a hallmark of advanced leadership development. The work and research of Bill Torbert[3] shows how leaders evolve in their ability to work with ambiguity, and to hold multiple perspectives to navigate complexity. These leaders learn to stand back – seeing the system as it is, making connections, and challenging to drive systemic change. The impact of this ripples through the ecosystem, leading to cultural shifts.

In Torbert's Action Logic framework, leaders evolve in how they relate to and manage doubt. At the earliest stages – the Opportunist and the Diplomat – doubt is avoided or dismissed. Further up the ladder, the Expert and the Achiever are technically confident and goal-driven, treating doubt as something to be overcome. It is only in the later stages – the Individualist and the Strategist – that leaders begin to harness doubt, questioning assumptions, making connections others may not see, and building followership through vision and trust.

Active Doubt is the developmental practice that can support this progression. In the context of systemic doubt, it asks leaders to view the whole system and not only its disparate parts.

Leaders create the environment for others to step up and see their own role in driving systemic change. To present it, and say – 'what do you think?'

How?

- We visibly role-model Active Doubt for the system.
- We think in systems, not people.
- We challenge the defaults – in meetings, metrics, and reviews – to surface invisible doubts.
- We embed structures that make challenge easier – building feedback loops, decision frameworks, and red flag routes that keep doubt alive in the system.

- We get the difference between Active Doubt and inactive doubt – challenging the system to work through it and not stall.

Leaders create the environment where doubt can be voiced, inviting others to step up, challenge assumptions, and see their role in driving systemic change.

Active Doubt is what happens when doubt makes a break for it, ventures out and demands to be heard and acted on. It is not dependent on heroic individuals; it flourishes when systems expect, enable, and protect it.

Moving doubt into action

A financial organization had been struggling with a stalled project for four years. That is four years of missing the opportunity to methodically address a rising tide of customer sentiment. The doubts and challenges had paralyzed them – is it the right approach? Is it the right metric? And even, whose responsibility is it?

The project, complex as it was, ran counter to the culture of the organization which was modern, nimble, and with a bias for action. The paralysis was unusual, and continuous, unprocessed concerns from team members stalled progress. Velocity was the only way out, detaching from the outcome.

Doubt wasn't the problem – it was the inaction around it. It swirled without structure.

The breakthrough came when the team reframed the goal: not to solve everything at once, but to focus on velocity rather than the outcome. They found the way to operationalize their doubts.

It wasn't about 'moving fast and breaking things.' It was about moving intentionally and keeping doubt in the room. Talking, tracking, delivering. Velocity became the vehicle for doubt to move – not stall.

This is Active Doubt in practice. Doubt was already there – but they hadn't found a way to collectively work with it. Velocity gave it a route into action.

Active Doubt is not dependent on heroic individuals; it flourishes when systems expect, enable, and protect it

Making systems doubt-responsive

Embedding doubt is not always about inventing new structures. Often it means taking the systems that already exist and adapting them so they respond to doubt rather than suppress it. Performance management is an example. In an auditing firm, the leadership were asking their partners to make a strategic shift to focus on long-term relationship-building – where the payoff might take a few years to come through. Doubt surfaced from their colleagues:

'Will I get paid for this?'

'Does this count?'

'Am I even good at it?'

Instead of ignoring the doubt or trying to 'motivate' people through it, they tracked it. They updated the year-end review process to clearly signal which behaviours would now be measured to focus on relationship-building. This is doubt, structured into the system.

In parallel, they also supported people and any self-doubts they may have had about their capability to do this work, by encouraging them to build on their strengths and partner with others who bring complementary ones. They were building rigour and guardrails into both the system and the self – creating the scaffolding that supports people to act.

How do we ensure Active Doubt is sustained?

Tracking 'good trouble'

We track engagement already. We need to extend this, to track engagement with doubt. Tracking ensures it is embedded into the culture. It gives data teeth to what can be viewed as subjective. The teeth of data sharpen the organization's focus on operationalizing systemic doubt. Asking the question sends a clear signal that doubt is welcome, that doubt is needed, and doubt needs to be actioned.

Statements to consider:

* I feel safe asking difficult questions and I know I will be listened to.

- I believe my thinking – especially when it challenges the status quo – is genuinely considered.

- Leaders here model openness to challenge and critique.

- In my team, we regularly and freely discuss differences of opinion.

The data collectively creates a doubt culture index, which can be monitored over time.

Rewarding 'good trouble'

If we want systemic challenge to thrive, we need to reward the act and not just the outcome. If something is noticed and rewarded, it will be replicated by other people.

How?

- Think doubt not outcome. Reinforce the act of speaking up, which is just as important as what results from it.

- Highlight the hero who has raised the red flag, and share the impact it had on the business.

- Call out when people share their doubts, listen to others' doubts, and turn them into Active Doubt.

- Feed back in individual reviews when people made 'good trouble', highlighting the impact it had.

- Shout out the process and not just the outcome. Highlight who raised the doubt that changed the course of the thinking, rather than simply focusing on the outcome.

Good trouble signals a healthy, striving, and productive culture. Harmony, on the other hand, might be a sign of fear. A place to start might be to doubt harmony itself. The irony is hard to ignore – a team at peace is a team at risk.

Active Doubt is intent on better, and the intent is to lead the future.

Sustain: tune into organizational signals

One Vice President I worked with was known for being grounded, authentic, and trusted – especially when it came to solving complex operational problems. He had a reputation for picking up the mess that others avoided, and he was energized by doing it. What frustrated him, though, were the more performative parts of the organization's culture – like a two-day planning meeting that included playing crazy golf and avoided talking about the elephants in the room, or a town hall meeting that felt like a PR exercise. These things pulled him away from the real issues, and the time spent in those spaces felt like a loss of traction, not a gain in clarity.

On the surface, this could have been about managing his frustrations and what he was feeling about the situation. Whilst I might have been able to help him feel differently about these, we would not have been working on the root cause of the frustration. What was underneath it was something else: systemic doubt. He wasn't doubting himself – he was questioning what the system valued. Why did it reward visibility and rituals over deep problem-solving? Why did it seek blame instead of collaboration to solve?

He also felt the weight of unspoken expectations. When he was disengaged, his director lost confidence in him. And in a high-blame culture, confidence was currency. But instead of resisting these situations or retreating in protest, we explored a different route: curiosity. Could he go into these spaces not to perform, but to listen – to observe the patterns, signals, and power dynamics at play? Could he use these moments not as interruptions, but as data points?

I suggested he imagine himself writing a book called *What the System Is Telling Me*. What would he notice if he tuned in differently, not to his frustration but to the mood in the room, the people who speak and those who don't, the unspoken rules of belonging and credibility?

Systemic doubt is often an invitation to read the room more deeply, not just react to it. He didn't need to start playing politics like others did. But he could start noticing the politics – and deciding how to show up with integrity within existing structures. It is the system which is driving these behaviours, not the people. The real power wasn't in opting out. It was in staying in, eyes open, and acting with choice.

Listening for doubt in the system takes alertness – not just attention, but a kind of spatial awareness. Listening for the patterns behind the person – the structures, incentives, and history shaping the words being spoken. The ability to hear the silence as much as the word.

The voice of the system

One helpful reframe is to listen for the voice of the system, and not for the voice of the person, as in the client example above.

Yes, it will be the person speaking, but what part of the system are they representing? What is the system trying to alert us to through the person?

Perhaps:

- A neglected stakeholder? A customer even?
- The 'ghost of the past'?
- A process that is being ignored?

When a junior analyst questions why we are still reporting on something that is no longer relevant, they are maybe carrying the voice of a future customer, or a process that is overdue for change.

The focus is on the content, not on the character. Not on who said it, but what is being said. It allows you to get underneath the surface of the words, bringing you closer to the root cause. It removes blame and judgment, allowing the person's thinking to be heard.

The stakeholder tangle: when avoiding conflict masks deeper doubt

We know we need to manage our stakeholders, but that is often easier to type than to do. I was team-coaching a public sector leadership team, where tensions were bubbling and the air between them was fraught. It felt personal. As always, it rarely is. In an early session we mapped out all their stakeholders, of which there were many, and many who could cause considerable challenge, which had the potential to be messy and public. By recognizing the complexity they faced together, they realized the challenge was external rather than between themselves. This lowered the tension a notch or two and fostered a sense of togetherness and shared purpose. The challenge, after all, was on the outside not on the inside. They had projected their doubt onto each other and neglected to see that it was caused by stakeholder complexity.

Instilling systemic doubt in team cadence

Surfacing unspoken doubt shouldn't be left to chance – it needs a rhythm. Structured reflection sessions can help teams to safely explore 'what is not being said.' Designating a rotating Chief Inquirer – someone who facilitates non-judgmental listening – creates a shared responsibility for doubt.

This is not therapy. It's systemic hygiene. Just like financial audits or risk reviews, doubt needs a standing slot. When built into quarterly reviews or offsites, these moments normalize openness and reinforce a culture of curiosity and challenge.

Systemic doubt distilled: leading with good trouble

- *Design for doubt.* Systems don't naturally invite challenge – we have to build it in. From Martha's Law to coaching cultures, the best organizations create clear, structured pathways for doubt to be voiced and heard.

- *Hire and promote for Active Doubt.* Look for leaders who reflect, question, and admit what they don't know. The sweet spot of doubt signals curiosity, humility, and readiness to lead complex systems with *integrity*.

- *Govern for challenge.* Boards and executive teams must act as guardians of doubt – creating the space for dissent, oversight, and tough questions. Tools like devil's advocacy and pre-mortems turn resistance into rigour.

- *Operationalize Active Doubt.* Don't just listen to doubt – track it, reward it, and build it into your culture. Whether through performance reviews, red flag systems, or feedback loops, doubt must be translated into decisions.

- *Reward 'good trouble.'* Celebrate not just results, but the courage to challenge. The raise is the win. When we reward principled dissent, we fuel a culture that improves itself – bravely, consistently, and together.

- *Listen systemically.* Don't just hear the person – hear the system speaking through them. Doubt can signal overlooked stakeholders, outdated assumptions, or invisible tensions. The real question is: what is the system trying to say?

Doubt, done well, is leadership. Making 'good trouble' is leadership.

Conclusion: Why we need to keep talking about doubt

The final line in John Patrick Shanley's play *Doubt: A Parable* is 'I have doubts.' After nearly two hours of escalating tensions, characters' inner conflicts, and institutions' unwillingness to doubt, doubt still remains.

And that is why we need to start and keep talking about it.

Doubt's 'work' is never done, and that is something we need to be grateful for. It's a force that creates change, and challenges us to be even better. Never before have we needed this quality more to meet the complexity and the opportunities of today.

Leaders doubt. They always have. But for too long, we haven't talked about it, or placed any value on it. And yet the most effective leaders don't eliminate doubt – they leverage it. They move with doubt. Doubt with purpose.

It is a leadership skill we need to recruit for, develop, and encourage.

Remember the leader at the start of this book – the one who considered quitting to open a coffee shop? She wasn't lacking competence. She was wrestling with self-doubt. But over time, she stopped trying to silence it. She started listening to what it was trying to tell her.

Take the moment she had to give an underperforming team member a poor rating. She feared pushback, that HR might see her as too harsh. But instead of letting fear paralyze her, she interrogated it. She checked her facts, consulted HR, and asked herself:

'If someone else were his line manager, what would they do?'

The answer came quickly: 'Exactly the same.'

That wasn't weakness. That was clarity.

Not confusion, but insight.

That wasn't self-doubt. It was situational doubt.

Wisdom in disguise.

When we add doubt as a leadership capability to our skillset, it not only matures our own leadership but that of the team, the organization, and the system as a whole.

The purpose of this labour of doubt – this book – has been to cast doubt on doubt itself. *To reclaim it as a force that can challenge, create, and collaborate, especially when coupled with courage.* Doubt left unspoken can stagnate. But Active Doubt is like water; flowing and shaping the system as it moves. It is the current that carries organizations forward, keeping them agile, honest and focused on better.

As we move further into the age of artificial intelligence, doubt must step up to meet the ethical and moral questions that demand scrutiny. Its role is not to halt progress, but to hold it accountable – to ensure choices serve the many, not just the few. We need to make space for doubt in organizations and systems, not as a handbrake, but as part of the solution. Because cultivating doubt as a leadership skill has never been more vital.

To brilliant doubting, and the flow of Active Doubt that moves us forward.

With thanks for the brilliance of others

This book has been a series of false starts and bumpy sticking points, demanding that I walk my talk on doubt. Yet, joy has come through the many people who journeyed with me, and to them I extend my heartfelt thanks.

This book was inspired by the original 'brilliant doubters' – my clients. They have actively and generously contributed their stories, thinking and offering encouragement along the way. It is always a great privilege to work alongside you. I am lucky to be in a profession I love, and I can't imagine doing anything else. Every day, I get to explore someone's thinking and bear witness to the adventures it takes us on. I may be full of doubt, but from my very first coaching session, I have never doubted that I was in the perfect lane for me. And that lane is full of brilliant doubters just like you. Thank you.

Alongside my clients were the people who kindly gave me time to understand their experiences of doubt, sharing their wisdom and constructive suggestions. The following people have their fingerprints all over this manuscript and contributed greatly to my thinking: Annabelle Baker, Clafoutie Sintive, Donald Morrison, Des Power, Gary Wilson, Heather Ang, Jeremy Borys,

Pam Burton, Pete Markey, Tony Miller, Rania Robertson, Simon Appell, Stephen Maher, Tim Coolican, and Visha Kudhail.

Whilst the coaching conference I attended was uninspiring, the choice of who I sat next to was inspired and that person was Sally Netherwood, a fellow coach. Without Sally there would be no book. We started writing our first books at the same time and have stumbled forward together. She has encouraged, supported, and listened to my phone moans to get me to the point of completion. If you are writing your first book, my one piece of advice is to get yourself a 'Sally' – it will make all the difference.

It was a big ask of those who willingly waded through my early drafts – with my half-baked thinking, jumpy flows, and prose that frankly needed a sledgehammer taken to it. The following are the brave and patient souls who did this for me: Harriet Brooke, Kirsty Cook, Mayur Soni, Natalie Malevsky, Rhona Moodly, Trias Kolokitha-Schmitz, and Yasmeen Cappuccini. I was blown away by your generosity of time, thought, and care.

All coaches need supervision, which is in fact a space for doubt to get to different thinking. And I have two brilliant supervisors, one for individual coaching and one for team coaching: Claire Pedrick and Dr Hilary Lines. Both took on the role of Chief Encourager and constantly offered thoughts and ideas to help shape my thinking on doubt. We all need wise women in our lives.

I also want to acknowledge Natalie March and Jodie Brock from Villain (www.wearevillain.com) who created my beautiful book cover. I am a visual person, and having a cover I loved early on helped to breathe life into the words when there were scant few. To Mike Mizen who helped convert scribbles into professional diagrams, and to his better half Nikki Woodford, who valiantly tries to keep me organized and structured. To Anna Kunst (www.annakunstphotography.com) who worked her magic as always.

To my relentlessly positive publisher – Alison Jones, who rightly ripped up my first suggestion for a book, and redirected my energy to where it should be. Alison has two superpowers: the spotter of good ideas in a sea of chaos and a surprising belief that eventually she would get her hands on my manuscript. To all at Practical Inspiration Publishing and Newgen, you have been patient, professional, and lovely to work with, and particular thanks to Michelle Charman who gave me an extra weekend to polish and refine. Michelle, I slept a little easier because of this, thank you.

To my parents, who have always – and remain – my biggest believers. You never doubted me, even when I doubted myself, and that quiet faith has carried me further than you know. Thank you for tolerating my writing woes and my quiet occupation of your dining room when I came home to write. To my clever, caring and dear friend Diane Lester, who went above and beyond in her encouragement, sharing her own thinking and wisdom which has found its way into these pages. To all my friends who firmly kept their hands on my back as I wrote – thank you, and especially you, Fra Houseman. For the public record, though, we are not reviewing this at book club.

Finally, to everyone who believes that doubt can be a force for good – this book is for you.

Notes

Introduction: why we need to talk about doubt

1   Ardern, J. *A Different Kind of Power: The Soft Skills of Leadership*. Penguin Random House New Zealand, 2024, p. 331.
2   'Doubt.' *Oxford English Dictionary*. 2nd ed., Oxford University Press, 1989.

As doubt grows: is certainty the answer?

1   Butler, S. 'Marks & Spencer Cyber-Attack Disrupts Deliveries as Online Orders Halted.' *The Guardian*, 30 April 2025, www.theguardian.com/business/2025/apr/30/marks-and-spencer-cyber-attack-products-run-short-in-some-stores
2   Erlick, N. *The Measure*. Harper, 2022.
3   Harari, Y. N. *Sapiens: A Brief History of Humankind*. Harper, 2015, p. 36.
4   Sharot, T. 'The Optimism Bias.' *TED Conferences*, July 2012, www.ted.com/talks/tali_sharot_the_optimism_bias
5   Reuters Institute for the Study of Journalism. *Digital News Report 2024*. University of Oxford, 2024, https://reutersinstitute.politics.ox.ac.uk/digital-news-report/2024
6   Harvard University's Human Flourishing Program and Gallup. *The Global Flourishing Study: 2025 Report*. Harvard University, 2025, https://globalflourishingstudy.com/wp-content/uploads/2025/04/GFS_Report.pdf
7   Nokia Corporation. *Nokia in 2007: Annual Report*. Nokia, 2008, www.nokia.com/system/files/files/request-nokia-in-2007-pdf.pdf
8   Edelman Trust Institute. *2025 Edelman Trust Barometer*. Edelman, January 2025, www.edelman.com/trust/2025/trust-barometer

9   Ahir, H., N. Bloom, and D. Furceri. 'The World Uncertainty Index.' *NBER Working Paper* no. 29763, National Bureau of Economic Research, October 2018. SSRN, https://ssrn.com/abstract=3275033
10 Edelman Trust Institute. *2025 Edelman Trust Barometer.*
11 Streeting, W. 'Assisted Dying Law Could Put Pressure on Patients to Save Money, Warns Health Secretary.' *The Guardian*, 13 November 2024, www.theguardian.com/politics/2024/nov/13/assisted-dying-law-nhs-cuts-wes-streeting

Doubt: a neglected discipline

1   'Antony Gormley Sculpture Installed at Wells Cathedral.' *BBC News*, 26 August 2021, www.bbc.co.uk/news/uk-england-bristol-58341947
2   'Antony Gormley Sculpture.' *BBC News.*
3   Heisenberg, W. *Physics and Philosophy: The Revolution in Modern Science.* Translated by A. J. Pomerans, Harper, 1958.
4   Moskowitz, C. 'It's Official: Neutrinos Can't Beat Speed of Light.' *Wired*, 8 June 2012, www.wired.com/2012/06/neutrinos-cant-beat-light/
5   Carson, R. *Silent Spring.* 40th Anniversary ed., introduction by L. Lear, Houghton Mifflin, 2002.
6   Descartes, R. *Discourse on the Method of Rightly Conducting the Reason, and Seeking Truth in the Sciences* [1637]. Translated by J. Veitch, Dover Publications, 2003.
7   Descartes, *Discourse on the Method*, 2003.
8   Beauvoir, S. de. *The Ethics of Ambiguity.* Translated by B. Frechtman, Citadel Press, 1948, p. 44.

The 'do' in doubt: Active Doubt

1   Gallup. *Global Leadership Report: What Followers Want.* Gallup, 2025.
2   Nissen-Lie, H. A., Hjeltnes, A., Ulvenes, P. G., Farber, B. A., and Stiles, T. C. 'Therapists' Professional Self-Doubt and Self-Compassion in the Context of a Challenging Therapeutic Process.' *Psychotherapy Research*, vol. 27, no. 5, 2017, pp. 595–605, https://onlinelibrary.wiley.com/doi/10.1002/cpp.1977

The doubtful self I: what shapes us

1   Haig, M. *The Midnight Library.* Canongate Books, 2020.
2   Williamson, M. *A Return to Love: Reflections on the Principles of 'A Course in Miracles.'* HarperCollins, 1992, p. 90.

The doubtful self II: how it speaks to us

1 Clance, P. R., and S. A. Imes. 'The Impostor Phenomenon in High Achieving Women: Dynamics and Therapeutic Intervention.' *Psychotherapy: Theory, Research & Practice*, vol. 15, no. 3, 1978, pp. 241–47, https://doi.org/10.1037/h0086006

2 Sakulku, J., and J. Alexander. 'The Impostor Phenomenon.' *International Journal of Behavioral Science*, vol. 6, no. 1, 2011, pp. 73–92.

3 Festinger, L. 'A Theory of Social Comparison Processes.' *Human Relations*, vol. 7, no. 2, 1954, pp. 117–40, https://doi.org/10.1177/001872675400700202

4 Young, V. *The Secret Thoughts of Successful Women: Why Capable People Suffer from the Impostor Syndrome and How to Thrive in Spite of It.* Crown Business, 2011.

5 Brown, B. *Atlas of the Heart: Mapping Meaningful Connection and the Language of Human Experience.* Vermilion, 2021.

The brilliant leader: how doubt unlocks leadership power

1 Booth, R. 'Michelle Obama Tells London School She Still Has Imposter Syndrome.' *The Guardian*, 3 December 2018, www.theguardian.com/us-news/2018/dec/03/michelle-obama-tells-london-school-she-still-has-imposter-syndrome

2 Pompliano, P. 'The Immortal Anthony Scaramucci.' *The Profile*, 4 February 2025, www.readtheprofile.com/p/the-immortal-anthony-scaramucci-profile

3 Maister, D. H., C. H. Green, and R. M. Galford. *The Trusted Advisor.* Free Press, 2000.

4 Spiro, R. J., W. Vispoel, J. Schmitz, A. Samarapungavan, and A. E. Boerger. 'Knowledge Acquisition for Application: Cognitive Flexibility and Transfer in Complex Content Domains.' *Executive Control Processes in Reading.* Ed. B. C. Britton and S. M. Glynn, Lawrence Erlbaum Associates, 1987, pp. 177–99.

5 Saïd Business School (University of Oxford) and Heidrick & Struggles. *The CEO Report: Embracing the Paradoxes of Leadership and the Power of Doubt.* April 2015, www.sbs.ox.ac.uk/sites/default/files/2018–09/The-CEO-Report-Final.pdf

6 Semple, S. 'David Bowie on Why You Should Never Play to the Gallery.' 12 May 2016, www.youtube.com/watch?v=cNbnef_eXBM

7 Gehry, F. 'Building Art: The Life and Work of Frank Gehry.' *Charlie Rose*, 11 December 2015, https://charlierose.com/videos/29150

8 Video interview between R. Robinson and J. Williams, 21 August 2024.

9 Bjork, E. L., and R. A. Bjork. 'Creating Desirable Difficulties to Enhance Learning.' In *Psychology and the Real World: Essays Illustrating Fundamental Contributions to Society*, edited by M. A. Gernsbacher et al., 2nd ed., Worth Publishers, 2014, pp. 59–68.

10   Tewfik, B. A. 'Workplace "Impostor Thoughts" May Have a Genuine Upside.' *MIT Sloan School of Management*, 15 April 2022.

11   Tewfik, B. A. 'The Impostor Phenomenon Revisited: Examining the Relationship between Workplace Impostor Thoughts and Interpersonal Effectiveness at Work.' *Academy of Management Journal*, vol. 65, no. 3, 2022, pp. 988–1018.

12   Grant, A. *Re:Thinking*, podcast, 25 October 2022, https://podcasts.apple. com/us/podcast/reese-witherspoon-on-turning-impostor-syndrome-into/ id1554567118?i=1000583714635

13   Video interview between R. Robinson and J. Williams, 21 August 2024.

The 'do' in self-doubt: how to FLOW through it

1   Popova, M. 'No Te Salves: A Poetic Invitation to Aliveness from Uruguay's Great Humanistic Voice.' *The Marginalian*, 10 January 2025, www.themargi nalian.org/2025/01/10/no-te-salves

2   Csikszentmihalyi, M. *Flow: The Psychology of Optimal Experience.* Harper Perennial Modern Classics, 2008, p. 4.

3   Csikszentmihalyi. *Flow.* p. 3.

4   Park, J. 'Conviction Is Key.' *RingCentral*, 13 March 2025, www.ringcentral. com/us/en/blog/startup-advice/

Situational doubt: when the questions come from the outside

1   Francis-Devine, B. 'Has Labour Market Data Become Less Reliable?' *House of Commons Library Insight*, 30 October 2023, https://commonslibrary. parliament.uk/has-labour-market-data-become-less-reliable

2   Wanous, J. P., A. E. Reichers, and J. T. Austin. 'Cynicism about Organizational Change: Measurement, Antecedents, and Correlates.' *Group & Organization Management*, vol. 25, no. 2, 2000, pp. 132–53.

Finding the brilliance: the power in situational doubt

1   Gormley, A. 'Doubt For Me is the Engine of Truth, and We Each Have to Make Our Own Truth.' *Wells Nub News*, 16 April 2022, https://wells.nub. news/news/local-news/antony-gormley-in-wells-103616

2   Interview between J. Borys and J. Williams, April 2025.

3   Farokhmanesh, M. 'Unity May Never Win Back the Developers It Lost in Its Fee Debacle.' *Wired*, 22 September 2023, www.wired.com/story/unity-walks-back-policies-lost-trust/

The 'do' in situational doubt I: how to steer through situational doubt

1   Edmondson, A. C. 'Psychological Safety and Learning Behavior in Work Teams.' *Administrative Science Quarterly*, vol. 44, no. 2, 1999, pp. 350–83.
2   Clark, T. R. *The 4 Stages of Psychological Safety: Defining the Path to Inclusion and Innovation*. Berrett-Koehler Publishers, 2020.
3   Trimboli, O. *How to Listen: Discover the Hidden Key to Better Communication*. Page Two Books, 2022.
4   Nepo, M. *Seven Thousand Ways to Listen: Staying Close to What Is Sacred*. Free Press, 2012, p. 6.
5   Prebble, L. Interview by Elizabeth Day. *Grazia*, no. 858, 13 June 2023, p. 27.

The 'do' in situational doubt II: turning doubt into wiser decisions

1   Sze, D. 'Why We Invested in LinkedIn Nine Years Ago.' *Fortune*, 15 October 2013, https://fortune.com/2013/10/15/why-we-invested-in-linkedin-nine-years-ago/
2   Strebulaev, I. A., and A. Dang. 'Make Decisions with a VC Mindset.' *Harvard Business Review*, May–June 2024, Harvard Business School Publishing, https://hbr.org/2024/05/make-decisions-with-a-vc-mindset
3   Trimboli, O. *How to Listen: Discover the Hidden Key to Better Communication*. Page Two Books, 2022, p. 68.
4   Kleiner, A. 'The Dilemma Doctors.' *Strategy+Business*, no. 23, 2001, www.strategy-business.com/article/17251?gko=444c1
5   Trompenaars, F., and C. Hampden-Turner. *Through the Looking Glass*. Shell Group, 1985. Cited in Art Kleiner, 'The Dilemma Doctors.' *Strategy+Business*, no. 23, 2001.

The invisible architecture: systemic drivers of doubt

1   Green, F., et al. *Dreaming Big: Self-Evaluations, Aspirations, High-Valued Social Networks, and the Private-School Earnings Premium*. UCL Institute of Education Centre for Learning and Life Chances in Knowledge Economies and Societies (LLAKES), Working Paper no. 2015/9, November 2015.
2   Heffernan, M. *Wilful Blindness: Why We Ignore the Obvious at Our Peril*. Simon & Schuster, 2011, pp. 44–45.
3   Wynn-Williams, S. *Careless People: A Story of Where I Used to Work*. HarperCollins, 2025.
4   Scharmer, C. O. *The Essentials of Theory U: Core Principles and Applications*. Berrett-Koehler Publishers, 2018.

5 Oshry, B. *Seeing Systems: Unlocking the Mysteries of Organizational Life*. 2nd ed., Berrett-Koehler Publishers, 2007.
6 Meadows, D. H. *Thinking in Systems: A Primer*. Chelsea Green Publishing, 2008, p. 164.

When the system is not brilliant: the power in doubt

1 McChrystal, S., et al. *Team of Teams: New Rules of Engagement for a Complex World*. Portfolio/Penguin, 2015, p. 123.
2 Hoffman, R., and G. Beato. *Superagency: What Could Possibly Go Right with Our AI Future*. Authors Equity, 2025.
3 Hern, A. 'Reid Hoffman: "Start Using AI Deeply. It Is a Huge Intelligence Amplifier."' *The Guardian*, 22 March 2025, www.theguardian.com/technology/2025/mar/22/reid-hoffman-superagency-start-using-ai-deeply-it-is-a-huge-intelligence-amplifier
4 Kegan, R., and L. Laskow Lahey. *Immunity to Change: How to Overcome It and Unlock the Potential in Yourself and Your Organization*. Harvard Business Press, 2009.

The 'do' in systemic doubt: good trouble

1 Harvard University. Congressman John Lewis Address/Harvard Commencement, 24 May 2018, https://www.youtube.com/watch?v=XRjAzepG-bA
2 Feigen, M. A., M. Jenkins, and A. Warendh. 'Is It Time to Consider Co-CEOs?' *Harvard Business Review*, July–August 2022, https://hbr.org/2022/07/is-it-time-to-consider-co-ceos
3 Torbert, W. R. *Action Inquiry: The Secret of Timely and Transforming Leadership*. Berrett-Koehler, 2004.

Index